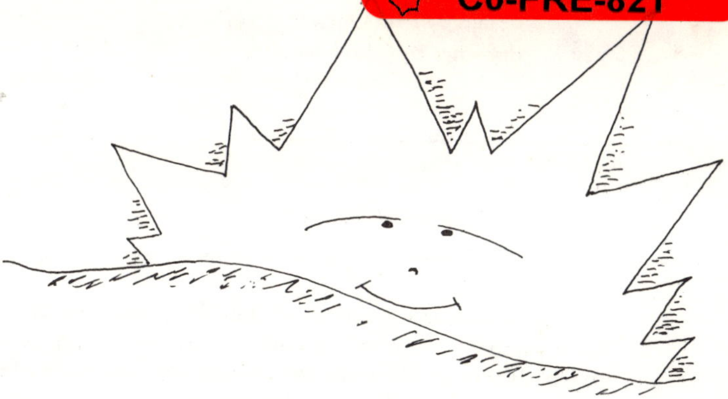

150 Plus!

Games and Activities for Early Childhood

Zane A. Spencer

Fearon Publishers, Inc., Belmont, California

edited by Judith Quinn
design by Paul Quin
drawings by John Hammett
and Bill Warrick

Acknowledgments

Books such as this are never written alone, and I would like to thank the many, many people who freely shared their ideas with me and generously gave of their time. Three teachers in particular were constant sources of inspiration, ideas, and encouragement. In my opinion they are not only master teachers, but also master people, and my special thanks go to: Harriet Arnold, kindergarten teacher, Dillon Elementary School, Carman School District, Flint, Michigan; Fran Williams, preschool story hour teacher, Flint Public Library; and Shirley Erber, special education teacher, Carman School District.

I am also greatly indebted to my kindergarten classes throughout the years at both Rankin Elementary School in the Carman District and Griffith Court Elementary School in the Bendle School District. It was with these children that most of the ideas in this book were tested.

"Strange Visitor," page 92, adapted from "The Strange Visitor," by Joseph Jacobs, in *Good Stories for Great Holidays*, by Frances J. Olcott, with the permission of Houghton Mifflin Company, Boston, Mass.

"From Valentines to Shamrocks," by Zane A. Spencer, page 119, reprinted with permission of the publishers, Allen Raymond, Inc., Darien, Conn. 06820, from the March 1973 issue of *Early Years*.

Recipe for potato latkes in "Latkes for Hanukkah," page 107, from *The Art of Jewish Cooking*, by Jennie Grossinger. Copyright ©1958 by Random House, Inc. Reprinted by permission of Random House, Inc.

ISBN-0-8224-5068-2
Library of Congress Catalog Card Number: 75-32842
Printed in the United States of America.

Contents

III Building Motor Skills 65

IV Special Days and Special Seasons 92

Introduction

Today children begin school with more knowledge than ever before in the history of education, and it is a truly exciting and challenging time for primary-school teachers. Some of the children are shy and a little afraid. Others are outgoing and precocious. Most are eager to learn and to explore the world of school. All of them are mixtures of pliable and individual personalities, differing in background, maturity, and abilities. The challenge for teachers is to work with their individual needs to promote the maximum total development of each child. Many studies have confirmed the theory that the best way to meet this challenge is to provide a program that includes a wide variety of learning experiences.

This book is designed as a practical handbook of games and activities that can enrich established curriculums with ideas for many kinds of experiences that can contribute to children's intellectual, social, emotional, and physical development. All of these games and activities have been tested in the classroom. Some of them are old. Some are new. All of them work. But, as every teacher knows, suggestions work best when they are used as a springboard or as a focus for the creativity of an individual teacher.

Specific goals and objectives are indicated at the beginning of each game or activity, but no attempt has been made to assign the projects to particular ages or levels of difficulty. At the primary level, this is far better left to teachers, whose daily contact with their students allows them to know both the group and the individual needs. With this knowledge of their students and with the aid of the variety of ideas presented here, teachers are encouraged to adapt the material, without any erroneous and inflexible instructions on exactly what a child should be doing at exactly what age. Just remember that children need to feel successful, which should be one of your most important guides in planning all activities in the classroom.

Dear Parents:

We are beginning a new school year, and I am very happy to have your child in my class. I feel a close relationship between parents and teacher is extremely important to your child's progress, so I am taking this opportunity to tell you a bit about what we will be doing at school. I hope to answer a few of the questions you may have, and I would like to encourage you to get in touch with me if you have any further questions or problems. (*Specify how, where, and what time you may be reached.*)

Supplies: (*Ask for any materials you wish children to bring from home to be kept at school, such as a painting smock or shirt, a box of tissues, or such.*)

Show and Tell: This is an important language experience for your child, and I will be encouraging all of the children to bring toys or other items from home to share with the class from time to time. Children should not bring anything they would be upset about if it should be broken or lost. You might encourage your child to bring things in a paper sack for easy handling. Also encourage your child to discuss the contribution with you in advance. While doing this, you might reinforce the habit of speaking in complete sentences, which I will be stressing here at school. For example, ask your child to say, "I want to take my car to school," rather than simply, "my car."

Boots and Outer Wear: As it upsets children to lose their belongings, please help by labeling all sweaters, coats, mittens, hats, boots, and such. Self-care will also be stressed at school, so please help your child to learn to zip, button, and put on his or her own boots and clothes.

Teachers, as well as children, benefit greatly from harmonious parent-teacher relationships. This is especially true at the primary level. The following suggestions and examples are included to help save you preparation time and to spark additional ideas for achieving a satisfying program of communication with parents:

Early in the school year send an introductory note to parents. In it you can explain some of the ways parents and teachers work together, and you can list any supplies you may want children to bring from home. Since you may want to cover a great many aspects of the school year in your letter, a short introductory paragraph followed by a topic-by-topic description (as on page *x*) will work well.

Continue your letter in this way, including all areas of concern to you. These might include requests for homeroom mothers; explanations of money the child will need for milk or other things; comments on school parties; safety; or a description and a general schedule for conferences.

Conferences with parents are a vital part of early-education programs. Face-to-face communication provides a warm and sympathetic occasion for evaluating a child's progress, and it allows both parents and teacher to gain insight into the child and his or her development.

Teachers should plan for conferences carefully, which is much easier to do if you have kept complete records. Some teachers find it helpful to have several examples of the child's work to show and discuss. However, probably the most important factor in a satisfactory conference is to remember that parents want to hear good things about their children. Praising the positive first can make any more difficult disclosures of problems easier and can make parents much readier to cooperate.

Encourage parents to ask questions and to seek conferences any time during the year when they feel a problem is developing. This kind of rapport often makes the difference between a mediocre school year for you and the children and a highly successful one.

Scheduling parent conferences can take time, especially if you must schedule several conferences within one or two days, as is specified in some contracts. You may find using a simple form like the one on page *xii* helpful.

This form can be sent home with the children. Ask for an early return. The next day is suggested, as this will allow you ample time to contact any parents who do not respond.

Dear______,

I have scheduled *date* from *time* for your conference. We will meet here in the classroom and will discuss *child's name* 's progress in school.

Please check and return this card to school with your child on or before *date you want the card returned* .

1 I can keep my scheduled conference.

2 Please arrange another day.

3 Transportation is a problem. Could you come to my home?

4 I cannot meet this schedule. Please send me a written report.

Sometimes it is necessary to substitute written reports for conferences. The example on page *xiii* leaves space for personal comments.

Parents often ask, "What can I do to help my child at home?" Most of them usually appreciate being asked by a teacher for help in a specific area. This gives them a feeling of being a part of their child's schooling, as well as some knowledge of what is going on in the curriculum. Their participation can be extremely helpful to you, especially if you take a little extra time to detail exactly what you want them to do at home.

For example, if you want them to help with alphabet training, you might begin like the sample at the bottom of page *xiii*. (Continue in this way, giving parents a definite idea of the method you use in the classroom. You might also ask them to start collecting pictures of creatures or objects whose names begin with the sounds of certain letters. Give them an example, such as a lion for the "singing sound" *L, l*. Suggest where they can find pictures, such as magazines, newspapers, and catalogs, and give them some ideas for using the pictures while they are talking with their children. You might include step-by-step instructions suggesting exactly what to say and indicating what their child's response might be. An explanation of why you are studying certain letters and sounds is also appreciated.)

STUDENT PROGRESS REPORT

Name ______________________________ Grade ______________________

School ______________________________ Date ______________________

This report is based upon your child's independent performance and does not indicate your child's standing in the group.

1 Your child's general attitude is:

2 Your child's general performance in skills we are studying is:

	Satisfactory Progress	Having Difficulty
reading readiness		
math (number concepts)		
listening skills		
speaking skills		
printing his or her name (small-motor development)		
color concepts		
independence (managing clothing, care of materials)		
other ____________________		

3 Additional comments:

_______________ Teacher

Dear Parents,

Throughout the year we will be studying the sounds of the following letters and groups of letters. Each letter has a sound and a name. The children will be taught them as follows:

Letter	Name	Sound
M m	em	The Yummy Good Sound
P p	pee	The Popcorn Sound
D d	dee	The Drum Sound

In other letters you might request help in having the children count and match objects. For example, you could suggest that parents encourage their children to count the members of the family and then match one plate, one chair, or one napkin to each member.

Number recognition can be reinforced at home, too, if parents understand the importance of posting handmade pictures of numbers on the refrigerator door or some other easily seen place, or of counting objects aloud as they move through their daily routines. (Mother might say, "I have one box of cereal," or, "Here are two eggs." Father might say, "This is page three of the newspaper," or, "I need four nails to finish this job.")

The ways parents can help at home are really endless. Most are willing to help, but often they simply do not know what to do or how to do it. There is a word of caution, however. Too much pressure should not be put on the home. This can be avoided by establishing a friendly, cooperative tone in your letters with simple explanations, details, and examples. A successful letter exerts no pressure on parents or children, but it does encourage parent involvement and cooperation.

Parents can also provide valuable aid to busy teachers in the classroom and on field trips. Getting volunteers at the primary level is seldom a problem, but it can be if a teacher accepts aid without careful thought about exactly what is expected. Make sure you know what you want done, and explain it fully to your helpers.

The following are ideas for using parents as volunteer aids in the classroom:

1 Parents can call other parents to help with parties, field trips, and other special projects.

2 Parents who have unusual jobs (or community jobs you are discussing) might be asked to come and talk with the children.

3 Parents who know how to do something special, who have special hobbies, or who come from other countries might be asked to come and talk with the class about those.

4 Fathers can be encouraged to come to school to help with such projects as building. This is especially valuable if several youngsters in the class come from one-parent, mother-oriented homes.

5 One or two mothers could be asked to greet other parents on conference days or on days when all parents are invited to school for special occasions.

6 Some parents enjoy working with children in classroom learning centers and do a nice job of it.

Ideas for enriching school programs are, indeed, everywhere. But ideas are only the beginning. They must be converted into action by enthusiastic and concerned teachers. Collections of successful ideas can be compiled as this has been, but, when all is said and done, the most any author can hope for is to make a book that will stimulate a teacher's own enthusiasm. That enthusiasm is what determines the true effectiveness of any method, theory, idea, or suggestion. Thus, it is your personal contribution of energy that is needed to make this the functional, practical, and helpful handbook it is intended to be.

I

The First Days of School

The first few days of school are extremely important to young children. Getting off on the "right" foot at school can set a good tone for the child's entire year. This is the time when teachers can establish classroom routine, when they can still children's fears about leaving home, and when they can make school a happy place for youngsters to go.

This chapter contains ideas for introducing classroom routines and activities which have successfully made good first impressions on young children. It offers suggestions for bulletin boards, for beginning the day, for classroom routine and discipline, and for building self-images. While many of the ideas are not new to education, they are being used with success by enthusiastic teachers, and I hope that meeting them in this collection will encourage you to experiment with some of the ones you may not have tried before. If they work well for you, you have added some beginning experiences to your personal teaching repertoire.

Bulletin Boards

1
Paper-Doll Greeting

OBJECTIVE recognizing names.

MATERIALS construction paper, black felt pen, scissors, and straight pins (one for each person in the room).

Ahead of time, cover a bulletin board with background paper. Make the title "WELCOME TO SCHOOL" with black felt pen or construction paper letters. Place a picture or a drawing of a school building in the middle. Cut a bright-colored paper doll to represent each child in your class. (Construction paper 9″ x 12″ folded in

quarters allows you to cut four at a time and makes the dolls about the right size.) Cut some extra dolls for unexpected arrivals. Cut one larger doll to represent the teacher. Print a child's name on each of the small dolls and your name on the larger doll. Print so the names can be read at a distance. Now arrange the dolls on the board so the "teacher" is next to the school and the "children" are approaching it.

When all the children arrive, ask them to sit in front of the bulletin board for roll call. Discuss the words in the title, and tell the children that you are welcoming them to school. Point out the teacher doll, and explain that your name is on it. Ask the children to repeat your name after you say it for them. Tell them that you are going to wear the doll to help them remember your name.

Next explain that each of them, too, has a doll on the bulletin board with his or her name on it, and as you call the roll, you will help them find their special dolls. Pin the paper dolls on each child as you find them, saying that this will help you remember their names.

Dolls can be replaced on the board before the children leave for home. Then the children can find their dolls the next day and wear them again during school.

2
Shapes

OBJECTIVES recognizing basic geometric shapes, and small-muscle development.

MATERIALS scissors, construction paper, crayons, 9″ x 12″ manila paper, and a stapler.

Prepare a bulletin board displaying the four basic geometric shapes (circle, triangle, square, and rectangle), each shape cut from a different-color sheet of 9″ x 12″ construction paper. Also cut a supply (one for each child) of miniature geometric shapes, with each small geometric figure being the same color as the large figure it matches.

Shape bulletin boards are eye-catching, and they make a useful teaching aid when it comes time to introduce the basic geometric shapes.

To do this, you might introduce the shapes one at a time. For example, on circle day, give each child a miniature circle. Ask who can find a large circle on the shape board. Discuss the circle. Have them make circles with their fingers. Have the children form a circle around you. Conclude the activity by giving each child a sheet of 9" x 12" manila paper. Have them use their crayons to make as many circles on the papers as they can. While they are doing this, you can staple the miniature cutout circles onto their papers. Suggest they take their papers home and talk about circles with their parents.

3
Colors

OBJECTIVE recognizing colors.

MATERIALS new red, green, yellow, blue, orange, and brown crayons (one each) and construction paper.

Colors can make another good first-impression bulletin board. And this display, too, can be used for teaching.

Tape real crayons (the basic six colors) under sheets of construction paper that match their colors. Print the names of the colors on the sheets of paper with black felt pen.

4
variation
Color-Match Game

Make a set of names of colors on flash cards. Hold one up, and ask the children if they can match it with a color on the bulletin board. Further matching can be done when children have their crayons on the table in front of them. Point to a color. Ask the children to find the crayon which matches that color.

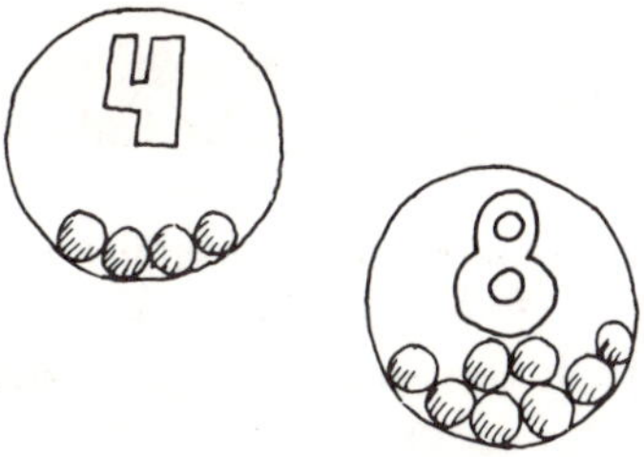

5
Numbers

OBJECTIVES recognizing numbers and concept development.

MATERIALS paper plates, black felt pen.

Cover a bulletin board with bright-colored background paper (red or yellow). Title it "CAN YOU COUNT?" Print numbers from 1 to 10, each on a paper plate with the appropriate number of dots representing the number. (Make two sets.)

Arrange one set of plates on the bulletin board. Use the second set for matching games similar to the one described in Activity 4.

Daily review of the numbers can be quickly done by asking the children to name each number as you point to it. And it is clear that several basic concepts can be reviewed with each of these boards. For example, you can review circle shapes and the color red (or yellow) when you are using the number board. You can count aloud the number of shapes on the board in Activity 2, and so forth.

6
The Calendar

OBJECTIVES recognizing numbers, practice in printing numbers, sequence, and building vocabulary.

MATERIALS a large calendar (about 18" x 24") made by the teacher.

Make a September calendar, and introduce a number a day, allowing a child to cross off the number of that day. As soon as you have introduced the children to printing numbers, make a blank calendar for the month, and choose a child each day to print the correct number of that date in the right spot.

7
Safety

OBJECTIVES developing the concept of safety.

MATERIALS free safety posters (available for schools from many businesses and service organizations, for example, the Bicycle Institute of America, Inc., 122 East 42d Street, New York, N.Y. 10017, or local fire departments).

Using the safety posters, plan a safety lesson to tie in with the bulletin-board display.

8
Autumn Pictures

OBJECTIVES developing language and introducing the concept of seasons.

MATERIALS pictures of autumn scenes cut from magazines.

Collect fall pictures, mount them on construction paper, and arrange them under the title "WELCOME SEPTEMBER." Talk about the fall season. Give the children an opportunity to discuss their experiences.

Get-Acquainted Activities

9

Begin the Day with a Fingerplay

OBJECTIVES developing classroom routine, good listening habits, fine-motor coordination, and auditory memory.

MATERIALS none.

One way to begin a school day is to follow a routine of sitting down together and saying a fingerplay. The following is an innovation on "Grandma's Spectacles."

This is my hat.
Make hat with fingers in an arc over head.

These are my glasses.
Make glasses frames around eyes with finger and thumb.

This is the way I fold my hands to begin my classes.
Fold hands in lap or on the table.

Innovating on fingerplays helps to develop children's creative thinking, as well as making some fingerplays more useful for specific teaching. Many excellent source books are available today.

10
Follow-the-Teacher Tour

OBJECTIVES developing independence and personal security, establishing rapport between teacher and students, and introducing words and setting the tone for recognition skills.

MATERIALS labels (attached to as many objects in the classroom as possible, such as desk, wall, floor, window, book, bulletin board, closet).

Help children to feel secure by familiarizing them with the classroom as soon in the school year as possible. Begin by introducing yourself:

> My name is_____ and I am your teacher. Can you say my name? Now you know who I am, and soon I will know who all of you are. I'm sure we are going to be very good friends. In fact, you are going to make a *lot* of new friends at school.

Continue your remarks, answering any apprehensive questions that may arise. Then explain that the classroom is a friendly place and that you would like all of them to play a game with you, called "Follow the Teacher." In this game you are the leader and you will introduce them to their classroom.

Begin the tour by making sure the children understand where the toilets and the drinking fountains are. Point to labels as you talk. Explain that the words stand for the things they label. Introduce work areas, play areas, bulletin boards, teacher's desk, the children's tables or desks, closets, coat racks, and supply-storage areas.

You can explain the rules regarding each area briefly as the tour proceeds:

> You will all have a chance to play with the toys, but we want to keep our room nice for everyone, so we must be very sure to put toys away when we've finished with them.

Young children accept rules very well and feel more secure about them if they are explained in a kind and reasonable way. Going to school is the beginning of independence for many children, and knowing what is expected there can be most important to them.

11
Inside Voices/Outside Voices

OBJECTIVES establishing classroom routine, developing personal responsibility, and building body images.

MATERIALS none.

Have the children sit in a circle on the floor. Make up a story about how people have two voices, or begin by asking the children questions such as, "How many hands do I have?" "How many hands do you have?" and "How many feet do I have?"

Continue by saying, "Did you know people have two voices too? One voice is very nice to use outside, and one voice is very nice to use inside. One voice is loud, and the other is quiet. Which one do you think is a person's inside voice? Why would your inside voice be better to use in our classroom?"

"Which voice am I using now?" "Yes, I try to remember always to use my inside voice inside, and I would like you to try to remember to do the same." You can explain why this is a good idea, giving several examples. The children will probably be able to contribute some examples of their own.

One way to encourage children to remember is to play a game of imagination with them. For example, have them line up outside after a play period. Ask them to take out their outside voices and put them in their pockets. Then ask them to look in their other pockets and take out their inside voices. Have them pretend to screw the voices into their mouths very tightly, because now it is time to go inside.

12
Our Flag

OBJECTIVES establishing classroom routine, developing auditory memory, and introducing the concept of and the history of the flag.

MATERIALS United States flag.

Introduce the flag to the children, and ask if anyone knows what it means. (Most young children haven't the slightest idea.) You can start with a simple explanation and then demonstrate the proper way to stand while saying the pledge. For example:

> The flag is the *symbol* of the union of fifty states and more than 200 million people in ONE country. We live in this country, and this is our flag.
>
> The stars in the flag stand for all the states. There is no one star for any one state, but there are fifty stars to stand for fifty states. The thirteen stripes (*The children can help count them*) stand for the thirteen original colonies that were here when our country began. The blue stands for justice. The red stands for courage. And the white stands for purity.
>
> When we say the pledge of allegiance to our flag, we stand up straight and tall and put our right hands on our hearts. (*Demonstrate, and ask the children to try it.*)

Learning to say the pledge is difficult for young children, but they can do it, with daily repetition. It takes much longer for them to understand all of the meaning behind the words, but a simple understanding of the respect of the symbol of their country can be established early and easily.

13

I Am Here

OBJECTIVES developing personal responsibility and name recognition.

MATERIALS a reading-pocket chart and blank index cards or tagboard strips about 3″ x 5″.

Print each child's name on an index card or on a sturdy strip of tagboard. Divide the pocket chart into two vertical sections with masking tape or a strip of construction paper. Label one side "I AM HOME" and the other "I AM HERE." Put the name cards into the "I AM HOME" side, and explain that each morning when the children arrive they will be responsible for taking their name cards from the home side and putting them into the here side. At first some children may need a little help both in remembering and in recognizing their names, but once the routine is established, it becomes automatic and fun. (A child's card is not in the same slot each time.)

Before the children go home, they can also put their name cards back in the "I AM HOME" side of the chart.

14

Keeping Track of Birthdays

OBJECTIVE building a positive self-image.

MATERIALS a poster or cutout picture of a birthday cake (about 18″ x 24″) with the words *happy birthday*.

At the beginning of the year, draw or make from construction paper a fairly large birthday cake. Display it in a place where it can be left all year. A wall, or perhaps the front of the teacher's desk, would save bulletin-board space.

Attach a chart that lists the birthdays of class members by month under the cake. You can set aside a special day each month to celebrate the birthdays of the children born in that month. Celebrate all summer birthdays in June.

If children offer you copies of their school pictures, you can display them around the birthday chart.

15

A Helping Verse

OBJECTIVES developing auditory memory, a positive self-image, responsibility, and language.

MATERIALS none.

To help children develop an awareness of themselves in relation to their families, as well as their new friends at school, teach the helper's verse, below. Then ask each child to identify the members of his or her family and tell how each of them uses helping hands at home.

Broaden the idea of helping at home to include all the ways they might help at school. This discussion could lead to organizing a plan for a room-helpers chart (Activity 16).

YOUR HELPING HANDS

Helping hands are hard to beat.
They make us happy and keep us neat.
Work is not so very hard if we share
Everyday and everywhere.

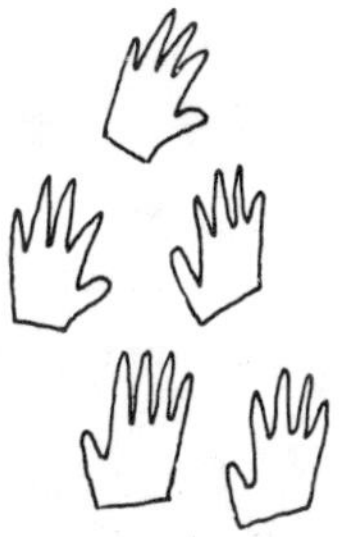

16

variation

Helping Hands at School

OBJECTIVES developing independence and personal responsibility.

MATERIALS 18" x 24" poster board or bulletin board, and picture symbols for classroom chores.

Discuss all the housekeeping chores that must be done each day in the classroom. Let the children name as many as they can. Then make a chart that everyone can "read," by using symbols or pictures to represent each chore.

Next, trace a child's hand on light-colored construction paper. Using this as a pattern, cut out a hand to represent each child. Print each child's name on a hand, and place each hand into the pocket opposite the chore that child is to do. The hands can be changed each week to give everyone a chance to help if there are more children than chores, or to give the children a change in chores.

17
Good Manners

OBJECTIVE social development.
MATERIALS none.

Good manners can best be explained and reinforced by example. When the teacher says "please" and "thank you," children soon respond in the same way.

Learning to say "I'm sorry" can be difficult for some children. Here again, a good example and a gentle reminder are usually all that is needed to establish an acceptable pattern of behavior.

Interrupting probably presents the most problems for teachers of young children. A firm but gentle attitude is about the only suggestion I can offer: "Please do not interrupt while I am speaking. Thank you." And, "You must wait your turn. It is now Johnny's turn to speak." Statements like these remind children that good manners involve waiting your turn and not interrupting while others are speaking.

This concept of good manners can be reinforced each day during "Show and Tell." In that activity they can plainly see that if they want others to listen while they are talking, they must also listen while the others speak.

18
Diagram of a Sneeze

OBJECTIVE developing good health habits.
MATERIALS chalk and chalkboard.

When the season for coughing and sneezing arrives, it can be helpful to draw a little diagram on the chalkboard.

Tell the children something like this: "Germs live inside coughs and sneezes, and they are very eager to get out and bother other people. Sometimes these little pests can make a person sick. This is

one way colds spread. You wouldn't want to make your friends at school sick, so don't share your germs. Be very careful to cover your mouth with a handkerchief or with your hand whenever you cough or sneeze."

19
Who, Me?

OBJECTIVE building a positive self-image.
MATERIALS hand mirror (optional).

To help children become aware of themselves as valuable people and to help build their self-images, play the game called "Who, Me?"

Have the children sit in a circle on the floor. Tell them that today all of you will have a turn to look at yourselves and say something nice about what you see. If you don't use a hand mirror, instead have each child take a turn to say at least one nice thing about himself or herself.

To give the children an idea of how to play the game, begin by saying something nice about yourself, such as, "My name is______, and I have a nice smile."

Hand the mirror to a child in the circle (or turn to the child), and ask the child to find something nice to say about himself or herself. If a child hesitates or can't think of anything to say, offer suggestions, like:

"Lisa has beautiful eyes."
"Mark has on a handsome plaid shirt."
"Joyce has pretty, long hair."
"Teresa has lovely white teeth."
"Bobby is friendly with everyone."

20
I Am Special

OBJECTIVE building a positive self-image.

MATERIALS 19″ x 12″ drawing paper (as many pieces as there are children); a felt pen; crayons for the children; paste; for each child two legs and two feet, two arms and two hands, one neck, and one head, each piece cut from 9″ x 12″ construction paper.

To encourage and develop self-awareness, have each child in turn tell one or two ways he or she is special. Make suggestions to those children who hesitate: "You make friends easily." "You sing well." "You paint lovely pictures."

Copy what each child says on a separate sheet of drawing paper and put his or her name on it. Then provide construction-paper cutouts of legs, arms, neck, and head, and show how the children can make a person to stand behind their stories, as illustrated. Have them use crayons to make special faces and then paste the parts to the sheets of drawing paper. The finished products can be displayed on a bulletin board or taken home.

Learning New Skills

21

I Think I Can

OBJECTIVES developing a positive self-image and fine-motor skills, and practice in printing names.

MATERIALS the book *The Little Engine That Could*, retold by Watty Piper (New York: Platt and Munk Co., Inc., 1961), and/or the film *The Little Engine That Could* (Chicago: Coronet Instructional Films, 1963).

Early in the school year tell the story or show the film of *The Little Engine That Could*. Follow with questions such as, "Did the little engine think he could make it up the hill, even though it was a very hard thing to do?" And "Do you think you could do things that may seem hard at first, if you tell yourself you think you can?"

Continue by telling the children they will be doing many new things at school. Tell them some things may seem hard at first but trying is the secret to success for them, just as it was for the little engine.

Have the children repeat the phrase "I think I can" several times. Then ask them to stand and hop on one foot or to perform some other simple task. Encourage them to observe that all of them are more likely to be able to do it when they try hard and if they think they can.

You might give other simple directions and then ask the children to try something more difficult. This would be a good introduction to having them try to print or trace their names. Remind them of the little engine and how he tried and tried again and, because he thought he could, pretty soon he did. If they try to print their names and believe they can, then someday soon they will be able to do it.

Each day ask the children to try to print their names on their drawing papers, their work papers, and all such. Remind them of the little engine, and reward those who try with a word of praise or perhaps some little prize like a raisin or marshmallow.

Children who succeed may print or trace their names on cards to be displayed on an "I Think I Can" chart.

22
Directions by Color

OBJECTIVES learning to recognize colors and following directions.

MATERIALS none.

Children can learn their colors in a hurry if the teacher begins a daily practice of giving directions to them by color. For example:

> "Will all the children wearing red please stand up? Those children may go to the circle first."
>
> "All children wearing blue may line up first for outside play."
>
> "If you have yellow on today, you may help sing the first song during music time."
>
> "If you are wearing green, stand up. You may get your hats and coats on first today."

To prevent any embarrassment of children who don't know their colors yet, you might gently suggest that a child look carefully at his or her shirt, for example. Then say something like, "That's a beautiful yellow shirt you have on. Did you forget that you wore your yellow shirt today?"

Other children are usually quick to help their friends, and they seem to do it in such a way that embarrassment is seldom a problem.

23
Making Math Practical

OBJECTIVES learning about numbers, social development, and gaining personal responsibility.

MATERIALS none.

Right away, start giving children opportunities to use math. During snack time, choose youngsters to count the people at their tables.

One child can be responsible for getting the right number of napkins; another, straws; and others, milk and cookies. Have them match the number of items to the children they are serving. If a child does not come out with the right number, have him say how many more he needs or how many he has left over. In this way, children not only gain practice in counting, but they also learn to be responsible for making adjustments.

variation

Another idea for making math practical is to choose a head-counter every day. This child walks around and points to each of the other children while the whole class counts aloud. Remind the head-counter to count himself or herself, too. Then, the child may put the number on the chalkboard, either alone or with help from the teacher. Next, have the head-counter add one for the teacher and announce, "We have the total number of people in our room today."

24
Introducing Scissors

OBJECTIVES learning safety skills, developing fine muscles, and identifying left-handed children.

MATERIALS a piece of paper for each child, scissors for each child and some left-handed scissors in addition.

Introduce the safe way to use scissors, and then give each child a pair, along with a large sheet of newsprint or construction paper. Ask them to cut out a very large circle. They can add a face with crayons after the circle is cut out. Demonstrate, to give the children the idea.

As they begin cutting, observe and note which children are right-handed and which are left-handed. You may wish to ask left-handed children to trade their scissors for a pair of "leftys." You can explain that the next time they cut, they should look for the scissors with the letters down the side. Those are the scissors that will make their cutting jobs easier.

25
Name-Printing Stands

OBJECTIVES developing small muscles and practice in printing names.

MATERIALS 1 sheet 9" x 12" construction paper for each child, and a felt pen for the teacher.

Fold sheets of 9" x 12" colored construction paper in half the long way. Print the children's names on white paper, and staple those strips to the construction-paper stands. You can either hand these out each day during name-practice time and collect them at the end of the period, or else you may want the children to keep them with their personal belongings and use them as they need to.

You might instead print each child's name on a strip of tagboard with felt pen. Place clear plastic over the strip, on which the children can trace the letters of their names with crayon. Later, the children can use the tagboard strips to look at while they practice printing their names on paper.

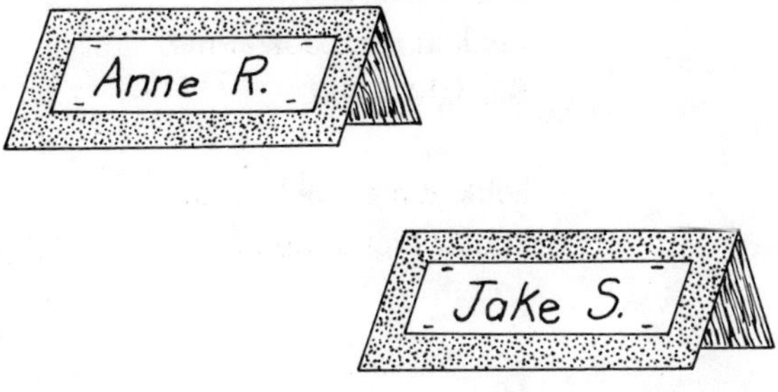

26
Look at Me

OBJECTIVES classroom management and developing large muscles.
MATERIALS none.

Sometimes when children are restless and need to be active before a quiet session of storytelling or before you give them some directions, try playing "Look at Me." The children enjoy this variation on the old "Teddy Bear, Teddy Bear" jump-rope rhyme.

Additional benefits include the development of motor control, exercise for large muscles, and an object lesson in the importance of listening to directions and following them.

Teach the poem, and demonstrate the actions that go with each line. Make the final line of the poem emphatic. Tell the children that when everyone is sitting down, it will be time to listen.

Look at me. Look at me.	*Point to self.*
Turn around.	*Turn around slowly as you speak.*
Look at me. Look at me.	
Touch the ground.	*Touch the floor.*
Look at me. Look at me.	
Show my toe.	*Point your toe.*
Look at me. Look at me.	
Round I go.	*Turn around.*
Look at me. Look at me.	
Jump my rope.	*Jump repeatedly.*
Look at me. Look at me.	
Wash with soap.	*Pretend to wash yourself.*
Look at me. Look at me.	
Sit right down.	*Children sit cross-legged on the floor.*
Look at me. Look at me.	
Shush! Not a sound.	*Put your finger to your lips, and be very still.*

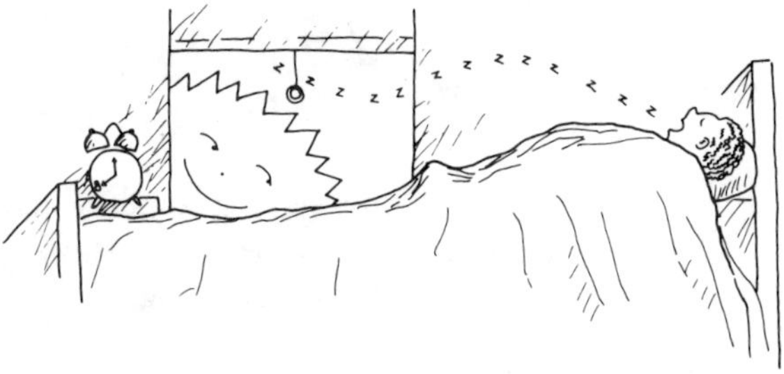

27
Singing in French

OBJECTIVES building a positive self-image, developing auditory memory, and understanding music.

MATERIALS piano.

Children enjoy learning something new, and they feel especially proud of themselves when they learn to sing a song in another language. Use the old folk song "Frère Jacques" to build this good feeling. The song is simple to translate and easy for the children to learn.

Frère Jacques, Frère Jacques,
Dormez-vous? Dormez-vous?
Sonnez les matines.
Sonnez les matines.
Din, din, don. Din, din, don.

When the children have learned the French version, translate it for them. Then ask them to sing it in English.

Brother John, Brother John
Are you sleeping? Are you sleeping?
The morning bells are ringing.
The morning bells are ringing.
Ding, ding, dong. Ding, ding, dong.

You might divide the class into two groups and have them sing the song as a round, one group in French and the other in English.

28

Introducing Role-Playing Kits

OBJECTIVES developing language and social studies enrichment.

MATERIALS whatever items fit into specific kits, and cardboard boxes for storage.

After a unit or discussion about jobs people do in the community or the world, you could use this follow-up activity for language development. Begin by introducing a box of role-playing materials for a specific job. (For example, a teacher kit might contain a pad of paper, a ruler, a piece of chalk, a chalkboard, flash cards, eyeglasses, crayons, scissors, and books.) Tell the children that you have included a few things a person doing that particular job might use at work. Ask if the children can think of other things that might be used in that job. Some of the children may volunteer to bring other items from home the next day. (Caution them to make sure they have their parents' permission.) Also, caution them regarding the safe use of materials such as the hammer and nails that might be found in a carpenter's kit.

After the children see what is in the kit, ask them to think of how they might play with it in the classroom. You might ask, "Could you make up little plays using all the things in the box? Sure you could. Let's make up a little play now." Select two or three children to begin. Help them get started by demonstrating some of the ways they could pretend to be working with the items in the kit.

Explain to the other children that they are the audience. This provides a good opportunity to talk about good audience behavior, such as listening, clapping at the end, and never booing at the people on stage.

When the first play is finished, other children may be chosen to make up another play using the same kit. Or you may wish to introduce a second kit for the second group of children.

Those kits could then be stacked in the corner of a drama learning center (or against any wall) and used during free-activity time.

The contents of your kits may be as simple or as detailed as you wish. Suggestions would be:

> The doctor or nurse: any items from toy doctor and nurse kits, cloth for bandages, tongue depressers, and empty pill bottles.

The actor: dress-up clothes, masks, makeup, mirror, wigs, props.

The chef: bowls, spoons, pans, apron, hat, other cooking equipment.

The beauty operator: combs, brushes, hair drier, curlers, ribbons, and mirror.

The plumber: wrenches and other tools, washers, an old faucet, a toolbox.

The explorer: pith helmets, parkas, old maps, compass.

The repair person: old radio or TV, clock, tools, hat.

The florist: Styrofoam bases, plastic flowers, ferns, bowls, vases, pots, ribbon.

The fisher: fishing poles, net, make-believe fish with magnetic bars.

The business person: briefcase, note pads, pencils, telephone, typewriter, appointment book.

29
Daily Evaluations

OBJECTIVES developing language and memory.

MATERIALS none.

At the end of each day, take a few minutes to recap with the class what has gone on. Encourage the children to discuss which activities they enjoyed most. They might also talk about any problems that arose and offer suggestions for avoiding similar problems in the future.

Questions you might use to encourage children to think and evaluate are:

> "Who can name some of the things we did at school today?"
>
> "Did we learn anything new?"
>
> "Did we hear a new song or listen to a new story?"
>
> "What special things did we practice today?"
>
> "What do you think was the most fun?"

Questions like these help young children to bring together the events of the day in their minds. They go home with a feeling of time enjoyed and time well spent.

II

Building Readiness Skills

From his experience in his activity school, John Dewey concluded that understanding and retention were greatly increased when children were provided immediate opportunities to use the skills they were learning. His conclusion has been supported by the observations of countless others since.

For preschool children, reading, writing, and the comprehension of mathematical concepts are still distant goals. Readiness to reach those goals involves many skills which can be strengthened through satisfying and successful enrichment experiences. At this level, as at other levels of education, conceptual learning tends to become more permanent when children feel they have good reasons for using their new knowledge. This chapter offers many suggestions for activities that will provide immediate and realistic use of the basic readiness skills.

30

Gentle Giraffes

OBJECTIVES recognizing geometric shapes, following directions, and learning letter sounds.

MATERIALS paste, crayons, scissors, 9″ x 12″ yellow construction paper (enough to cut giraffe parts for each child and for one demonstration giraffe, ahead of time).

To review and reinforce their recognition of geometric shapes, let the children use some of those shapes to make animals. You might correlate this activity with the introduction of letters and sounds, as well. For example, the gentle giraffe gives a good opportunity to enrich their practice of the soft sound of *G* and to reinforce their familiarity with the rectangle.

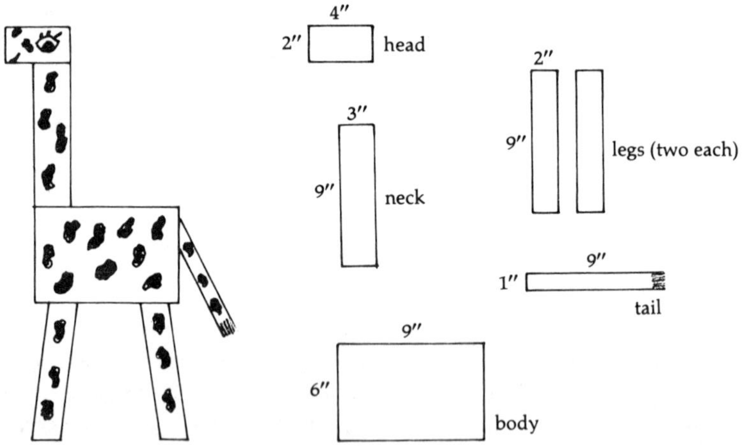

Cut the parts in advance. Choose one child to distribute a head rectangle to each other child. Choose other children to pass out the other pieces. When the children have all the parts of their giraffes, show a sample of an assembled giraffe (on a bulletin board or pasted on cardboard backing), and ask the children to arrange the pieces they have in the same way. Then they can paste them together. Have them use dark crayons to color spots and make a big, pretty eye on each head. Before attaching the tail, cut one end to give it a fringed effect.

Peppy Penguin

Happy Hippo

Zippy Zebra

Jumping Jumbo

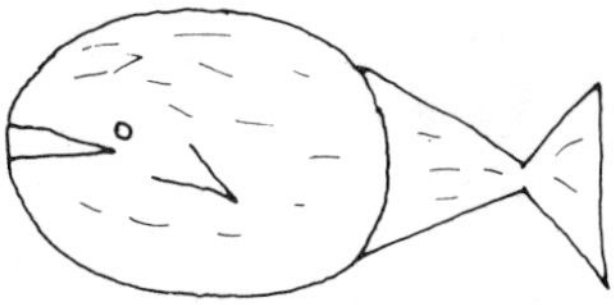

Whopping Whale

31

Going Places with Shapes

OBJECTIVES reinforcing recognition of geometric shapes, developing small muscles, and enriching a social studies unit.

MATERIALS duplicated sheets with outline drawings of vehicles discussed in a social studies unit on transportation (one vehicle per sheet, several sheets for each child), 9″ x 12″ construction paper (two for each child), crayons, and a stapler

This activity can be used to correlate a review of geometric shapes with a social studies unit on transportation. Give the children duplicated pictures of each vehicle as you discuss it with the components represented by geometric shapes. Talk about what shapes the children can find in each design. Then have them color the pictures and save them until they finish the unit. The children can then put all of their vehicle pictures together in a booklet.

To make booklets, give each child two sheets of colored construction paper for covers. Explain that they are to gather all their vehicle pictures, making sure the pictures are all right side up. When they have placed the pictures between the cover sheets, you can staple them down the left side, using two or three staples.

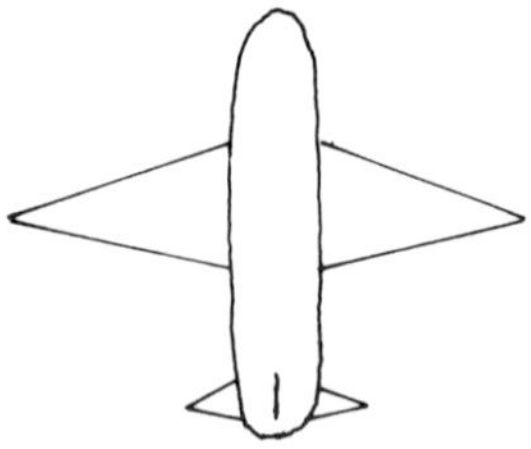

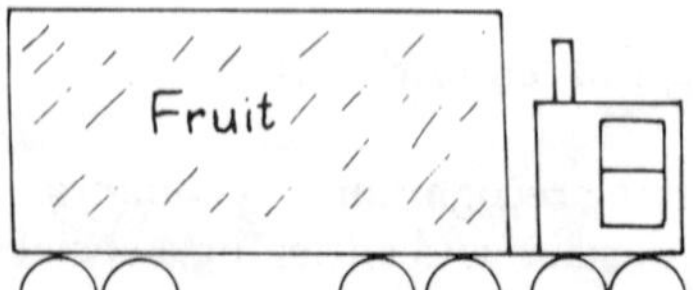

Other modes of transportation you could draw might include: feet, buses, cars, bicycles, motorbikes, roller skates, horses, campers, sleds, and ice skates.

32
Color Collage

OBJECTIVES recognizing colors and developing small muscles.

MATERIALS one 12″ x 18″ sheet of drawing paper per child, scissors, paste, magazines and catalogs with colorful pictures, and crayons for the teacher.

You can reinforce color recognition and fine-muscle development at one time with color collages.

Using crayons corresponding to the colors, print the names of colors on sheets of drawing paper, one color per sheet, and one sheet for each child. Explain that the word at the top of the sheet each child has is the name for the color that child is to look for. The child is to cut out and paste on the sheet of paper pictures of things of that color.

You might then keep a supply of materials for making color collages in an independent-activity corner, and post a chart of colors with their names printed beside them. Explain that children can choose to make more color collages. They may select a color and print its name at the top of their paper before they begin to cut and paste.

33
Classifying by Color

OBJECTIVES recognizing colors and developing visual discrimination.

MATERIALS two matching sets of color cards.

Make two sets of color cards of 9″ x 12″ construction paper. In each set have one of each of the nine basic colors (red, green, blue, brown, yellow, orange, purple, black, and white). Print the name of the color on each card, using a black felt pen.

Spread the cards on a table. Point to one color, and ask whether anyone can find a card from the second set that is the same color.

Continue doing this with different colors until the children understand what to do. Then ask if anyone can match all the colors. Let any child who can match all the colors successfully play teacher. Give him or her the first set of color cards, and allow another person to come up to the table and try to match them with the second set.

When a child has trouble, offer help and encourage the child to practice individually with you or with another capable child at other times during the day.

34
Classifying by Shape

OBJECTIVES recognizing geometric shapes and developing visual discrimination.

MATERIALS two matching sets of shape cards.

Using 4″ x 8″ index cards, make two matching sets of cards with the basic geometric shapes painted or drawn on them. Explain, and play the game described in Activity 33.

35
Classifying by Numbers and Letters

OBJECTIVES recognizing numbers and letters and developing visual discrimination.

MATERIALS two matching sets of letters and numbers cards.

Using 4″ x 8″ index cards, make two sets with matching numbers and two sets with matching letters. (The number of cards in each set is optional.) Black felt pen shows up well and helps you make simple matching sets quickly.

After the children become familiar with the game of classifying colors and shapes (Activities 33 and 34), the same activity can be used to reinforce number and color recognition.

36
Classifying by Size

OBJECTIVES developing visual discrimination and quantitative thinking.

MATERIALS at least six pairs of objects that are alike in every way except size (a large box and a small box of one brand of cereal, a teaspoon and a tablespoon, copies of the same book in hardback and paperback, a plate and a saucer, a big pencil and a little pencil).

Hold up two matching items. Ask which is smaller. Discuss the concepts of smaller and larger and then ask if someone could place all of the small items on one side of the table. Someone else might be asked to place all of the large items on the other side. This kind of activity reinforces the vocabulary needed for quantitative thinking that will be used in developing the concepts of mathematics in the future.

37

Squashing Shapes

OBJECTIVES recognizing geometric shapes and developing visual discrimination.

MATERIALS a crayon and a piece of paper for each child.

To reinforce their recognition of geometric shapes, give each child a sheet of drawing paper and a crayon. Draw a rectangle on the chalkboard, and point out its characteristics. Ask the children to each draw a rectangle.

Next, tell the children that you are going to squash your rectangle. Draw a horizontally elongated rectangle under the first one. Ask the children whether the squashed rectangle is still a rectangle. Ask, "Does it have four corners?" and so forth.

Then ask the children to draw squashed rectangles under the first ones they have drawn. Explain that they must be very careful to give their rectangles four corners, just as you have yours.

When they have finished and they have the idea, ask them to draw: a tall rectangle, a fat rectangle, a skinny rectangle, and whatever others come to mind.

Continue the discussion by asking the children to look for rectangles in the classroom (books, tabletops, windows, chalkboard).

38

Finding Mr. Different

OBJECTIVE developing visual discrimination.

MATERIALS half a dozen strips of tagboard (4″ x 10″) on which there are sets of six items with one item that doesn't match the others (see illustration) or duplicated sheets (one per child) with six to ten similar sets of items on each sheet.

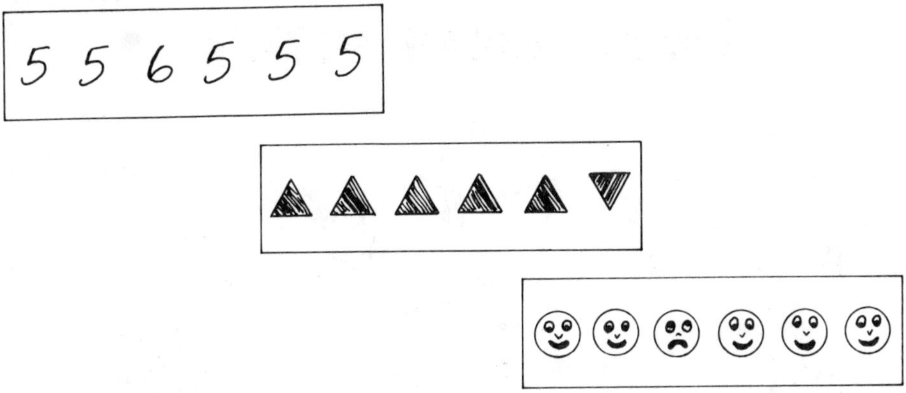

Make a set of strips which can be put in a pocket chart or on the ledge of your chalkboard, or prepare a set of duplicated sheets to give out to the children for individual practice. On each card make a set of pictures or symbols that are all the same with one exception (on each sheet make several sets). The exception is Mr. Different. Ask the children to find Mr. Different. Ask the children to find Mr. Different and explain how he differs from the others in that set. If they are working with duplicated pages, you can ask them to circle Mr. Different after the discussion.

39
How Many Fish?

OBJECTIVES recognizing numbers and practicing counting.

MATERIALS construction paper for fish cutouts and lettering for bulletin board.

For practice in counting and to help the children in recognizing numbers, make a bulletin-board fishbowl. Put one fish in it the first day. Ask the children to count the fish.

Add one or two fish each day, and count them all each day. One child can be chosen to count and tell whether any new fish have been added to the fishbowl.

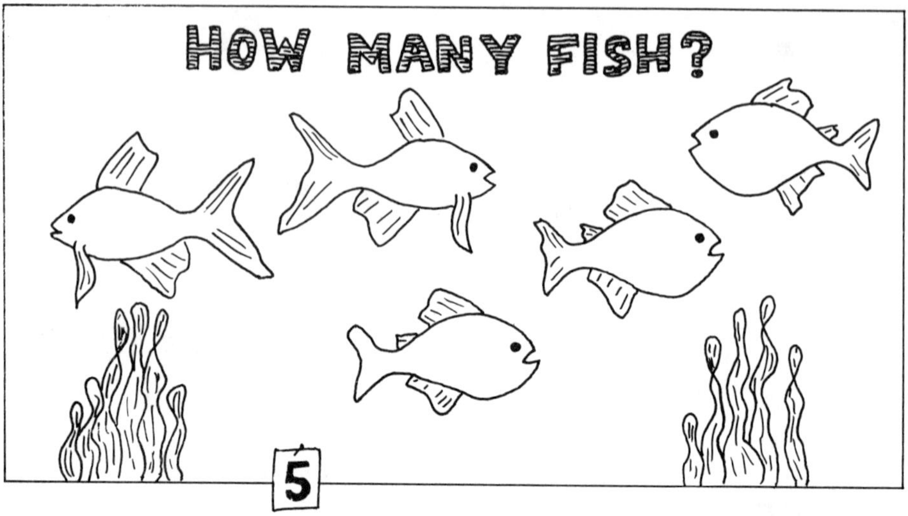

variation

Make a set of numbers on slips of white drawing paper with a black felt pen. After the fish have been counted each day, help the children select the slip that bears the number of the total, and let a child thumbtack it to the bottom of the fishbowl.

When ten fish (or whatever number you choose) have been added, you can take all the fish away and start over again.

40
Comparing Numbers

OBJECTIVES understanding numbers and developing quantitative thinking.

MATERIALS varied.

There are many ways to illustrate the comparison of numbers. Some of the activities children enjoy most are the following.

41

variation

Flannel-Board Figures

Use sets of matching commercial flannel symbols or make your own in simple geometric shapes. Place one set of symbols on the board, along with another set of another number of different symbols. Ask, "Are there as many trees as there are hearts?"

After the idea of comparing the numbers has been established, individual children may be chosen to select sets of symbols and ask the questions about them. As the game goes on, you might display more than two sets at once.

42

variation

Real-Object Lessons

Use sets of real objects for comparison, such as chairs, tables, books, chalk, crayons, and toys.

43

variation

Sets of Children

Line up a set of boys on one side of the room and a set of girls on the other. Determine how many are in each set, and ask the children to compare the numbers.

44

variation

Comparing in Riddles

Make up some silly riddles of comparison for the children to answer, and encourage them to make up their own riddles. For example, "Which is larger in number, one elephant or ten mice?" And then, "Which is larger in weight?"

45

Four on the Floor

OBJECTIVES recognizing numbers and developing muscles.

MATERIALS chalk, masking tape, and floor space.

A variety of number games can be played on a simple number board on the floor. To make a board, use masking tape to section off an area of squares. (If your classroom floor has a large circle painted on it, use that area.) Put a number in each square with chalk, in random order. The size and pattern of the board would have to be determined by the amount of space available in the room.

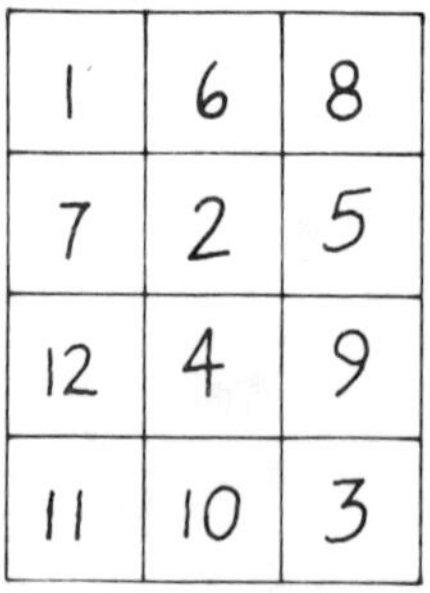

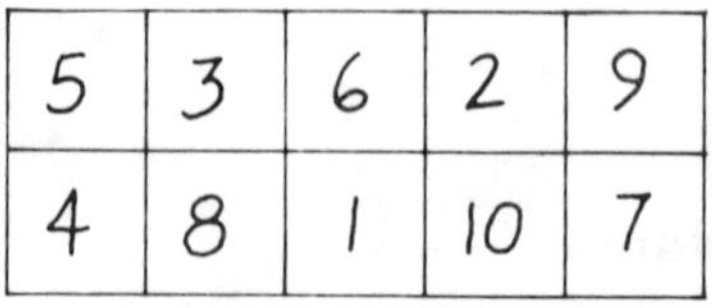

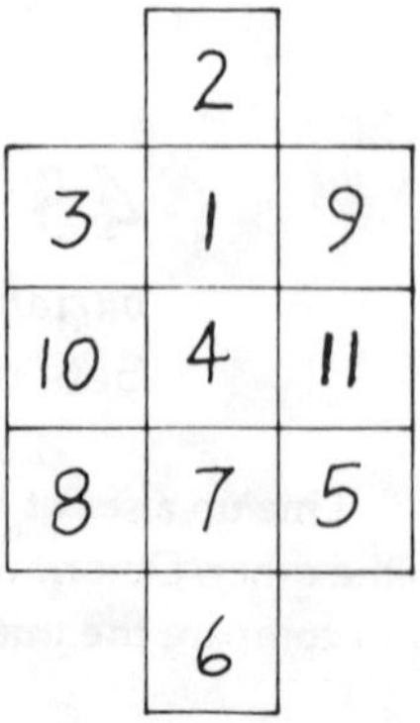

46
variation
Number Race

Two children stand ready for the call of a number from the teacher. When the number is called, both children race to the square containing that number. The winner (the one who gets there first) may receive a point or may be permitted to remain in the game until he loses to a challenger. Players can be asked to hop to the numbers or skip or jump.

47
variation
Backward Number Toss

Choose a child to stand with his or her back to the game board. (Or divide the class into teams, whose representatives stand at the board in turn.) Give the child a beanbag, and ask the child to toss it over his or her head so that it lands on the number board on the floor. The child then turns around to face the board and names the number upon which the beanbag has landed. If the bag has landed on a line, the child must identify all the numbers whose squares the bag is in. The child, or that team, receives one point for each correct identification.

48
variation
Call the Shot

One child faces the number board on the floor, and the teacher or another child calls out a number for the child to hit with the beanbag. If the child can toss the beanbag into that square, he or she gets one point. Then it is another child's turn.

49

variation

Hide and Seek

All the children, except one, who has been chosen to be It, close their eyes. Then, It goes to the game board and sits on a number, or hides the number with his or her hands. The other children open their eyes, look carefully at the board and try to guess which number is being hidden. If they guess right, a new It is chosen. If no one can guess, the same It gets to try again.

50

variation

Up and Down

The children take turns trying to hop on the numbers in sequence from the lowest to the highest, and then back down again. A child who goes all the way up and all the way down again, is a winner. The class may clap for winners, or the winners may receive stars or some other small rewards.

51

Symbol Show-offs

OBJECTIVES understanding numbers and developing quantitative thinking.

MATERIALS thirty 4″ x 8″ index cards (white) and assorted felt pens.

Make two sets of ten index cards each, with symbols on each card representing a number from 1 to 10 (one star, two balls, three trees, four flowers, five triangles, six boats, or the like). Do not have the sets match; use different symbols for each number. Also make a set of cards, one for each numeral between 1 and 10.

The children can match the cards bearing the same number values. That is, three boats and three flowers and the numeral 3. Or you might ask them to find the number card that means three and then match it to the cards that show three symbols.

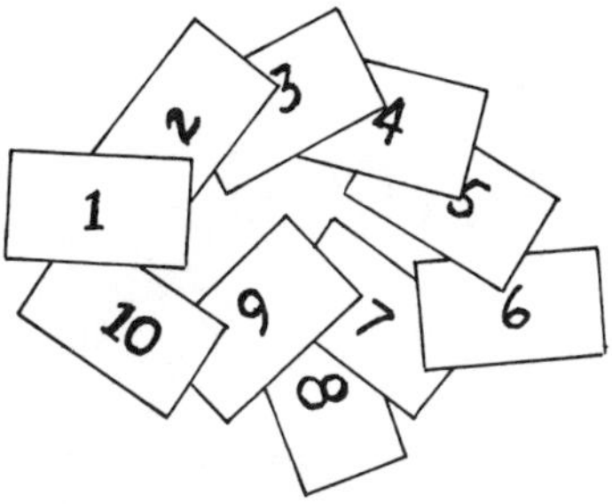

variations

Make this a Halloween or Christmas game by using symbols appropriate to the holidays. Or cut out attractive symbols from magazines or catalogs and paste them on cards. You might also laminate the cards, to create a more permanent teaching tool.

52
Can You Guess?

OBJECTIVES developing memory and visual perception.

MATERIALS an overhead projector, a screen (or a blank wall) and various small items such as a pencil, chalk, crayon, key, ring, and paper cutouts.

Have the children sit in a group in front of the screen or a blank wall. Place two or three items in the overhead projector. Have the children count the images they see on the screen. Then turn off the projector, add or remove an item, turn the projector back on, and ask the children to guess whether something has been added or whether something is missing.

As the children gain proficiency, two or three items can be added or subtracted at once.

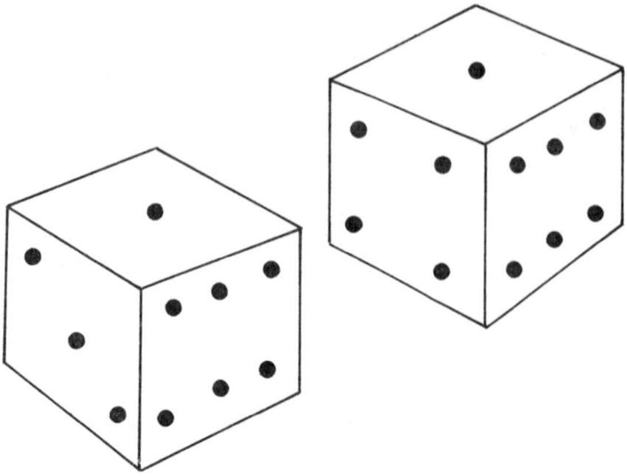

53

Big Dice Counting

OBJECTIVES developing quantitative thinking, reinforcing math concepts, and using waiting time well.

MATERIALS cardboard, masking tape, felt pen.

Make some oversize dice of sturdy cardboard, or paint two blocks of wood to resemble dice. They should be large enough for the children to see easily but small enough to handle and manipulate (about 5″ x 5″ x 5″).

Hold the dice together, and let the children count the dots on both. Reverse them, and have the children count again. Repeat until the children grasp the idea that $2 + 3 = 5$, and $3 + 2 = 5$, as well, for example.

This is a good activity while waiting for a bell to ring, for a visitor to come, or whenever you have only a few minutes.

54

Masking-Tape Math Strips

OBJECTIVES reinforcing addition and subtraction.

MATERIALS rulers (one for each child) covered with masking tape sticky side up (held in place by reversed tabs underneath) and twelve drinking straws for each child.

Give each child a tape-covered ruler and twelve drinking straws. Have them stick the straws to the tape, approximately one to each inch.

When this is done, the math lesson can begin. For example, write 1 + 1 on the chalkboard. Tell the children that the first number tells how many straws to take first from their math strips. When they see the plus sign, they know the second number tells how many more straws to take from the strip. Have the children do that and then ask, "How many straws do you have in your hands? . . . Yes, the answer to this problem is 2." Have them replace the straws on the strips.

Next, try subtraction. For example, write 3 - 1 on the chalkboard. Explain that the first number tells again how many straws to take from the math strips. The minus sign tells them to put some of those straws back on the tape (or to take them away from those in their hands). The second number tells them how many straws to put back on the tape. Put one straw back, and the answer to the problem is 2 (the number of straws in the hand).

55
Bottle Tops and Butter Cups

OBJECTIVES recognizing numbers and practicing counting.

MATERIALS ten or twelve margarine containers, a black felt pen, and enough tops from soda pop bottles to equal the numbers written on the containers.

An interesting math game for an activity center can be made with ten or twelve plastic margarine containers. Use a felt pen to write a number on each one. Save soda pop bottle caps, enough to match the numbers on all the cups. Put the caps into another container near the margarine cups.

Suggest that during free-activity time the children might like to see whether they can play a game with reading the numbers on the cups. First they read the number on a cup, and then they count out that many bottle caps and drop them in the cup. Post an I CAN DO IT chart, and when the teacher sees that a child is successful, his or her name is added to the chart.

56

Look and See November

OBJECTIVES developing visual discrimination, recognizing letters, and developing a concept of time.

MATERIALS calendar, chalkboard, white and one color chalk, duplicated sheets headed "Look and See November" with the words *No, Number, Monday, Orange, Thanksgiving,* and *Name* (with room for the child's name after it) printed large below the heading (one sheet per child), and a red crayon for each child.

Print the word *November* on the chalkboard. Explain that this is the name of the new month and that the word *November* will be used to help them learn to play a game called "Look and See November." You could tear October from the calendar at this point and discuss the calendar briefly.

Point to the letters in *November,* and help the children understand that all words are made up of letters. Some have lots of letters, others only a few. Count the letters in *November*. Count those in *October* for comparison.

Discuss the fact that *November* begins with a capital *N*. Look again at *October*. Does it have a big *N* in it? Let the children discover that it does not.

Put the name of the day on the board. Explain what the word names. "This is Monday," for example. "Can you find an *N* in Monday?" Explain the difference between a little *n* and a big *N*.

Print the names of some of the children on the board. Look for *N*s in their names. Circle them with colored chalk.

After the children have the idea of circling the *N*s in words, hand out a duplicated sheet and a red crayon to each child. Explain that now they are ready to play "Look and See November" all by themselves. Read the words on the list. Caution the children to look carefully at each letter in each word. Ask them to circle in red all the *n*s they can find. Remind them not to forget little *n*s that may be in the middles or at the ends of some words.

Collect their papers when they have finished. Check them, and praise those who have done well. Make plans to help children who need it.

57

Alphabet Fill-ins

OBJECTIVE developing auditory discrimination.

MATERIALS none.

Make up some riddles in which the answer (the final word) contains the sound of the letter(s) you are discussing. Say the riddle without the answer, and ask the children to fill in the missing word.

CH I have four legs. You sit on me.
I am a______. (*chair*)

I lay eggs for your breakfast.
I am a______. (*chicken*)

I go to school. I want to learn to read.
I am a______. (*child*)

I am brown and sweet and good to eat. Some candy bars are made out of me.
I am______. (*chocolate*)

Other *ch* words are: *church, cherub, cherry, chain, chilly, chief, children, chalk,* and *cheek.*

58

Alphabet Riddles

OBJECTIVES developing auditory discrimination and language.

MATERIALS none.

Children love riddles, and the riddles provide a good way to give the children practice in pronouncing the sounds of the letters they are learning. After you introduce each letter, tell a few riddles you've made up. Then ask the children to make up some riddles of their own. For example:

B I am round and I can be bounced up and down.
What am I? (*ball*)

I am little. I can't walk, and I need my diaper changed.
What am I? (*baby*)

I have two covers. Pictures and words are inside me.
What am I? (*book*)

P I'm not red, and I'm not white.
What color am I? (*pink*)

Your mother tells you not to walk in me because I get your feet all wet.
What am I? (*puddle*)

I hang on the wall, and people like to look at me.
What am I? (*picture*)

59
Life-Size Alphabet People

OBJECTIVES developing language and motor skills, and reinforcing knowledge of letters.

MATERIALS butcher paper as long as a child is tall (enough for each child), liquid poster paint, pie tins and jars or cups for paint, brushes, sponges, crayons, felt pens, scissors, scraps of construction paper, yarn, wallpaper, and white glue.

Pour several colors of poster paint into separate shallow pie tins. Fill each pan approximately one-fourth full. Put paint to be applied with brushes in jars or cups. Have sponges for applying the paint near the pie tins. Put a box full of colored paper, yarn, and wallpaper where they can be reached easily.

In large classes it is better to divide the class into three or four groups. Assign a letter of the alphabet at random to each group.

One child in each group is chosen to lie down on a large sheet of butcher paper. Another child then draws an outline around him or her with a crayon or felt pen. They take turns till everyone has been outlined. Before they cut the figures out, the children decorate their alphabet people. This may be done any way they choose, with paint or whatever material they need from the scrap box.

Either give the children their letters cut from construction paper (about six inches high) to paste on their figures' chests or print the letters on the figures' chests with felt pen.

60
Learning to Look

OBJECTIVE developing visual discrimination.

MATERIALS duplicated sheets with an incomplete picture on each (one per child).

To develop greater independence and to aid children in sharpening their powers of observation, duplicate incomplete pictures similar to the ones shown here. Give each child a picture, and ask the class to look carefully at the ones they have. Tell them, "Something is wrong with each of these pictures. Can you guess what it is? Can you fix your picture? Draw in the missing part, and then color the picture, if you like."

Another time make other pictures with something missing, to reinforce this practice in careful observation. Later you can use more difficult ones.

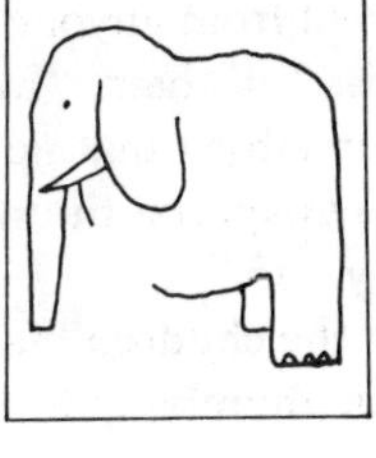

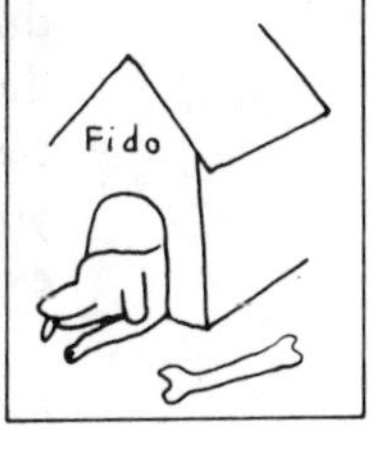

61

Funny Reading

OBJECTIVES developing reading readiness and the concept of reading from left to right.

MATERIALS a familiar book.

When teaching children to read from left to right, explain that this is how words are printed in our language. You might also tell them that some children in other countries (like China) learn to read and write from top to bottom but here we learn to read the lines from left to right, or the words will not make sense.

Select a passage from one of the children's favorite books. Now, ask the children to listen carefully because you are going to read something to them from right to left. Read the words in two or three lines in reverse order, and ask the children how they like listening to a story that way. Ask them what happened in the story and how it sounded to them.

62

Thumbprints

OBJECTIVES developing visual discrimination and language, and building a positive self-image.

MATERIALS half a sheet of 9" x 12" white drawing paper per child, an ink pad, a crayon for each child, and a wet cloth for cleaning the thumbs.

Begin by telling the children that each one of them has something that is different from anyone else in the world. Ask them to hold up their thumbs. Tell them, "Everyone has a thumb, but your thumb can make something that no one else's can. Your thumb can make your very own special thumbprint. No one else has a thumbprint exactly like yours."

Then give the children their drawing papers and show them how to press their thumbs onto the ink pad to make thumbprints. Let

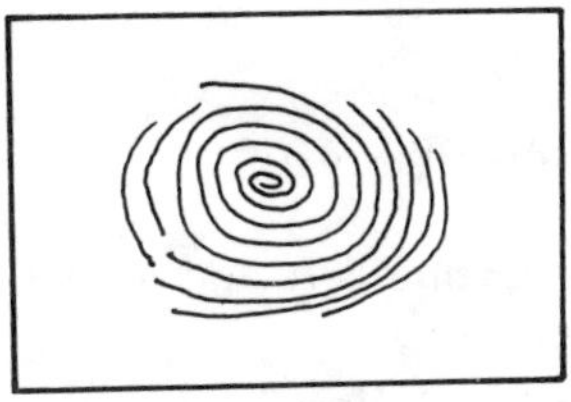
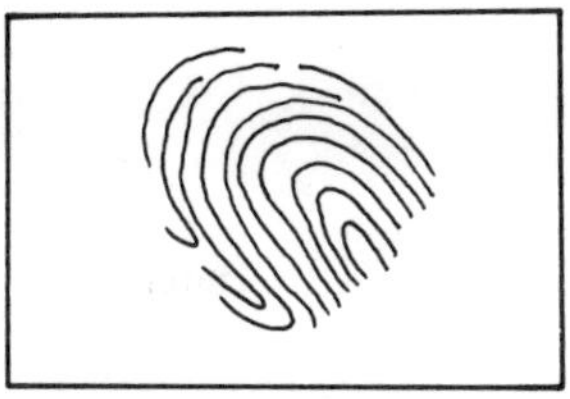

them compare their thumbprints and help them to see how they differ. Have them use their crayons to print their names on their papers and then take their thumbprints home to show their parents.

63

Action Match

OBJECTIVES developing visual discrimination and memory.

MATERIALS twelve or fifteen pictures from old magazines, tagboard strips (about 3″ x 10″), construction paper or tagboard for mounting the pictures.

In advance cut out twelve or fifteen pictures of people engaged in different active pursuits from old magazines or workbooks. Mount each picture on a separate sheet of construction paper or tagboard. On 3″ x 10″ strips of tagboard print the simple word for the action taking place in each picture, such as, *play*, *jump*, *swim*, *fly*, *run*, *skip*, *sail*, and *skate*.

Introduce the words and the pictures together. For example, hold up a picture and ask, "What are the children doing in this action picture?" When they answer, "playing," say, "Yes, this is an action picture about play. This is the word that says 'play'." Introduce the tagboard strip and place it by the picture.

Introduce two or three word-and-picture pairs each day. Review previously introduced pairs by letting the children match the words to the pictures. When the whole set has been introduced, the children can then play matching games with each other during free-activity time.

64

E-Z Reading Game

OBJECTIVES reinforcing numbers and letters, and developing visual discrimination.

MATERIALS chalk and chalkboard.

Write the following on the chalkboard. Explain that you have put a secret message on the board. Before the children can find out what the message says, all of the *x*s must be erased.

Choose one child to erase all the *x*s in the top row. Continue, choosing a different child to erase the *x*s in each of the other three lines. When all the *x*s are erased, ask if anyone can read the secret message now.

2 X X Y S X U X R X X
X 2 X X Y S X U X X B
I X C X X U X X R X X
2 X X Y S X 4 X X M E !

65

Letter Bags

OBJECTIVES recognizing letters and developing language.

MATERIALS paper sacks and construction-paper letters of the alphabet or a felt pen.

Use twenty-six paper sacks with a letter on each to introduce the letters of the alphabet. Either cut the letters from bright-colored construction paper and staple them to the outsides of the bags, or print the letters on the bags with felt pen.

As you introduce each letter, attach the corresponding paper bag to the bulletin board, leaving the bag open so you can drop things into it. Explain that it is the *B* bag, for example. Ask, "What things have names that start with *B* that we could put into the *B* bag?" (Examples would be a ball, another bag, a bottle, a blue paper, a black pencil, and a brown crayon.)

Ask the children to look for things at home whose names start with *B*. Suggest that they look for pictures in magazines and newspapers. Caution them not to bring anything to school without discussing it with their parents.

You might tack the letter bags to the bottom of a large bulletin board to save space and to make them easy to reach. And you might prefer to introduce one group of letters first and then, after a time, take those bags down to make room for a new group.

Spend a few minutes each day letting the children explain what they have brought, what letters those things start with, and what bags they will put them in.

66
Letter Letters

OBJECTIVES developing language and fine-motor skills, and recognizing letters.

MATERIALS butcher paper for large letters, old magazines, and scissors for each child.

Another good idea to use in addition to or in place of "Letter Bags" (Activity 65) is to cut very large letters from butcher paper. Mount one of the letters on a bulletin board, and then ask the children to cut pictures from old magazines of things whose names begin with that letter. When they find appropriate pictures, staple or paste them to the large letter.

67
Belling the Cat

OBJECTIVES recognizing letters, numbers, or words.

MATERIALS flash cards and a bell for each child.

This game is designed to spice up alphabet or word drills. The children sit in a circle, which encloses a "*nest*." Each child gets a turn to identify a letter or word the teacher shows on a flash card. If the child identifies it correctly, the child remains in the circle and is a *cat*. If the child misses, he or she hops into the center of the circle and becomes a *bird* in the *nest*. The cats may tell the name of the letter or word that was missed as the child goes into the nest.

The birds must perch quietly in the center of the nest until the teacher has gone all the way around the circle, giving each child a turn at naming a letter or word.

Then, the cats left on the rim of the circle get bells and prowl around the birds meowing and shaking the bells. This frightens the birds, who flap their wings and chirp loudly at the cats.

This is such an exciting game it is usually wise to include a rule that after the cats have prowled around the circle once or twice, they and the birds must go back to their tables and "sleep" until the teacher has counted to 100 slowly.

When weather permits, this game can be played nicely outdoors.

68
Lost Letters

OBJECTIVES recognizing letters and colors.

MATERIALS simple duplicated outline pictures containing hidden letters (five for each child), and crayons for each child.

Using simple outline drawings of trains, houses, barns, dolls, toys, and such, similar to the examples here, make pictures (one to a page) with hidden letters in them.

As a review to reinforce letter recognition, give the children one picture a day for a week to find the hidden letters in. Ask them to trace or circle as many letters as they can find. On the first day, demonstrate the procedure. Once the children know how to play the game, they are eager to see how many lost letters they can find in each new picture. (To help them with recognizing colors, suggest one day that they use red crayons and another day that they use green, and so forth.)

A, U, B, N, X, H, V, L, O, D

U, L, X, V, H, J, E, A, C, M

O, C, D, Z, I, H, G, P

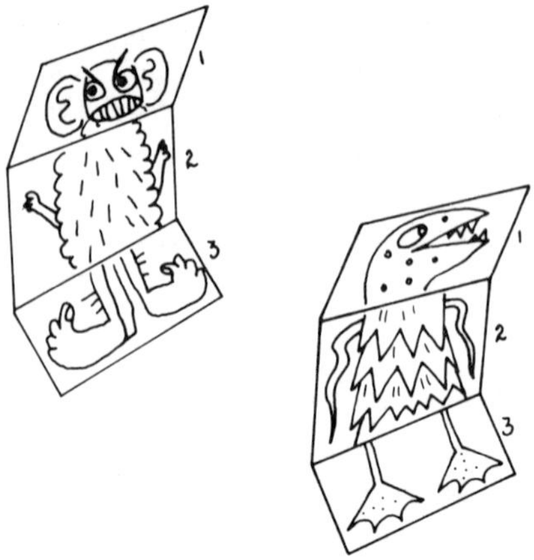

69

Creepy Creatures

OBJECTIVES developing language and fine muscles.

MATERIALS one sheet of 12″ x 18″ drawing paper and crayons for each child.

October is a good time to make creepy creatures, but the activity can be done anytime during the year. Have the children sit in a circle or around their tables. Give each child a crayon and a sheet of drawing paper folded in thirds across the short way. Caution them not to open the paper. Then tell them to draw a creepy creature head on the top surface. When they finish, have them turn that surface under so the next person can't see the head they have drawn. Now each child passes his or her paper to the child on the left. Everyone then draws a creepy creature body on the middle surface. (The first child draws little lines on the fold to indicate where the body attaches. The second child indicates where to attach the legs.) When the bodies are finished, fold and pass the papers along again. The third child completes the creepy creature by drawing legs on the final surface.

After all the creepy creatures are finished, the children can take turns opening the papers up. Give each an opportunity to show a creature and tell a creepy story about it.

70
Make a "Feely" Book

OBJECTIVE developing language.
MATERIALS hardcover scrapbook or loose-leaf notebook.

Young children need to talk, and they need to feel that others are interested in what they are saying.

One tool that can promote language development is a "feely" book. Making one requires some time and creativity from the teacher, but the results are well worth it, especially as the teacher can use the book over and over again with different classes.

Each "feely" book is unique, as there are no specific requirements for what to include. The point is to have a collection of pictures and materials children can express their feelings about. It may include pictures from calendars and magazines, textured fabrics or other materials, or anything else that might stimulate responses.

Introduce your book to the class by sharing some of your own feelings about the things on the first few pages. This will give the children an idea of the purpose. Encourage them to tell how a certain page makes them feel or to speak of how one picture reminds them of something else.

After using the book with the group, you can leave it in the reading center or on a bookshelf for use during free-activity time. Encourage the children to look at it in pairs or small groups so they can share their feelings with others.

71
Time to Eat

OBJECTIVES developing language and good nutrition.
MATERIALS pictures of foods mounted on construction paper and a paper plate for each child.

This activity provides an excellent opportunity to combine language development with a discussion of healthy eating habits. Using paper plates adds a game quality to the activity that most children enjoy.

Make a fairly large collection of pictures of individual foods. Provide a paper plate for each child. Introduce the pictures with complete sentences. For example: "This is corn-on-the-cob." "These are scrambled eggs." "This is an apple." Encourage the children to follow that example as they play the game.

Begin by telling the children you will place one of the pictures of food on each of their plates. Display the extra pictures on the chalk ledge. Ask the children to name what they have on their plates, using complete sentences.

Continue until the children can recognize and name the foods in all the pictures. A discussion of healthy eating habits could follow. Then, individual children could try selecting foods for complete meals using the remaining pictures on the chalk ledge.

72
Stand up, Mr. Opposite

OBJECTIVE developing language.

MATERIALS none.

After defining the word *opposite,* tell the children that you will say a word. If they can think of a word that is opposite to your word, they may stand up. Then ask each child who stands up to say his opposite word. Ask the class, for example, "Did Jerry think of an opposite word?"

The children are to answer (in complete sentences) either, "Yes, *day* is the opposite of *night,*" or "No, *breakfast* is not the opposite of *night.*" At that point, all the children who answered *day* may sit down. Explain the word *opposite* to those whose answers weren't opposite, and remind them they will have a chance to try again on the next word.

Possible opposites: *hot/cold, up/down, right/wrong* (or *right/left*), *laugh/cry, walk/run, happy/sad, early/late, fat/thin, good/bad, sweet/sour, big/little, short/long* (or *tall*), and *kind/mean.*

73

Shake, Rattle, and Roll

OBJECTIVES developing auditory perception and memory.

MATERIALS noisemakers.

Collect a set of noise-making objects, such as baby rattles, scissors, marbles in a bag, a paper sack, a horn, a whistle, two sticks, seeds in a jar, pages in a book to riffle, and lids of cooking pots to clang together.

Introduce three of the objects to the class. Make noises with them, and then let the children experiment with making the noises. When the children are familiar with the sounds, have them all close their

eyes. Select one object. Make its sound and ask them which object they heard. After they answer, they open their eyes to see whether they were right.

Give another example, and repeat the question. Gradually add new objects to the set, explaining each time that you are going to add something new. If the children can't guess what it is, let them open their eyes and look. Tell them you are going to put that object back with the other things and try it again later.

74
variation
Your Own Sounds

On another day, work with sounds the children can make themselves, such as clapping, stamping, tongue clicking, whistling, various animal sounds, and high and low voices. Have them close their eyes and listen carefully. Then have them try to reproduce the sound they heard.

75
Smelly Boxes

OBJECTIVE developing sensory perception.

MATERIALS several plastic containers filled with materials that have definite smells.

Collect several little plastic containers and fill them with various substances the children can smell. Put them all together in a box with a lid. Ask the children to open a container and sniff, and then guess what they are smelling.

Suggestions for ingredients would be: lemon, pepper, soap, after-shave lotion, perfume, garlic, vanilla extract, toothpaste, strawberry Jello, banana extract, maple extract, and mouthwash.

For a few days after the introduction of the "smelly box," you can set aside time each day to discuss the importance of smell. Those children who would like to can bring surprise contributions from home (with their parents' permission). Those children could pass their "smelly bottles" around for the other children to guess what is inside. Afterwards, add their contributions to the "smelly collection." (The collection should be kept only a week.)

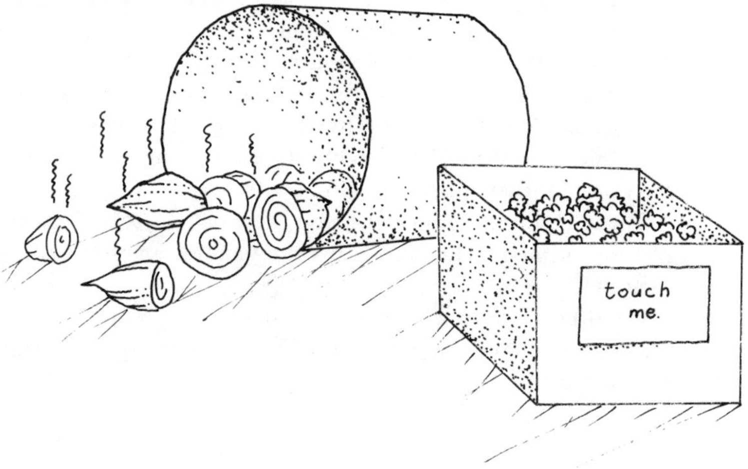

76
variation
Touchy Boxes

Use the same idea to discuss the sense of touch. Put small samples of "touchy" material into small boxes. Ask the children to touch them. Have them express how the various things feel to them and discuss the differences. Possibilities for a "touchy" collection are: sandpaper, popcorn (cooked), sand, salt, hair, clay lumps, olive oil, wool, fur, wadded tinfoil, cotton batting, and wadded paper.

77

Pet Parade

OBJECTIVE developing language.

MATERIALS pets, drawing paper and crayons for those without pets.

Select a day for a pet parade. Discuss with the children various rules and plans for the day.

Be sure to plan an hour when parents can bring the pets to school and take them home afterwards (first thing in the morning or last hour of the day are good). Send a note to parents asking if they will cooperate in transporting the animals, and inviting them to stay and listen while the children tell about their pets.

Tell the children that each one who brings a pet will have an opportunity to talk about it. They should give the pet's name and tell something about it. They might tell funny things that happened to their pets, or they might explain how they care for them.

Those children who can't bring their pets to school might draw pictures of them. They can show the pictures when they tell about their pets.

Children who do not have pets may draw pictures of pets they might like to have someday and tell why they think they might like to have them.

78

A Letter to Us

OBJECTIVES developing language and social studies skills.

MATERIALS letter paper, envelope, pen, and a stamp.

Enrich a social studies lesson on the post office by helping the class write and mail a letter to itself. The letter could be something like the sample below. Point out that it must be mailed in an envelope. Envelopes protect letters and keep the messages private. Promote a discussion on why this could be important. Discuss the way an

Dear Us,

Today we are writing a letter to ourselves. We are going to mail it and wait for the mailperson to deliver it to us. When we get it, we will look at the envelope to see what the post office did to it.

Love,

All of us

envelope must look and why the things written on it are there (return address, name, street address, city, state, zip code). Talk about the cost of a stamp and what kinds of things that stamp helps pay for (salaries of people who work in the post office, mail trucks, gas, and various other forms of transportation and equipment).

Make a trip to a mailbox or post office to mail the letter. When it is delivered, discuss how the envelope looks now. "What did the post office do to our letter?" "Does the stamp look different?" "What does the date on the envelope tell us?" "Notice that the city's name is on the envelope too." "What day did we mail it?" "What day was it stamped?" "What day is this?"

79

Pencil-Shaving Pictures

OBJECTIVES ecology enrichment and developing art skills.

MATERIALS paper, pencil shavings, and white glue.

To enrich an ecology lesson and provide the children with an interesting art activity, try making pictures with pencil shavings. You will need to save the shavings from the pencil sharpener for a few days in advance.

Discuss ecology and what it means to live in a world where all creatures and other things depend on each other. Explain that it is important to preserve the natural resources and not waste them. One way to do this is to find uses for things that we usually throw away.

Then introduce the art activity by saying, "Today we are going to make use of something we usually throw away. We are going to make pictures with pencil shavings."

Give each child a sheet of drawing paper or colored construction paper. They may share bottles of white glue and squeeze out designs with the glue on their papers. Demonstrate, so the children will know about how much glue to use (make the lines about as thick as a regular pencil).

When they have made their designs in glue, ask them to raise their hands. Then sprinkle or shake some shavings onto the paper. Tell the children to let the pictures sit for a minute and then shake off the excess into a wastepaper basket.

80

What Will I Be?

OBJECTIVES developing social studies skills and language, and building a positive self-image.

MATERIALS old magazines, drawing paper or newsprint, scissors, paste or glue, felt pen.

Cover a bulletin board with bright background paper and title it "WHAT WILL I BE?"

A social studies unit on the kinds of work people do can easily lead to a discussion of careers the children might like to follow when they grow up. This kind of discussion helps to build their self-images as well as giving them an additional opportunity to use language, which is so important to future reading ability.

After the children have had some time to think about careers and what they might like to do when they grow up, ask them to look through some old magazines to see if each of them can find a picture (or several pictures if anyone might like to do more than one thing) to represent his or her career. Then, have them cut the pictures out and paste them on sheets of newsprint or drawing paper. Tell them to make up stories about the pictures they have selected and you will print it below the picture.

81
variation
Career Bulletin Board

OBJECTIVES developing language and recognizing the alphabet.

MATERIALS 5″ or 6″ high construction-paper letters of the alphabet and pictures of people at work.

Prepare a bulletin board titled, "What Will I Be from A to Z?" Arrange large cutouts of the letters of the alphabet and magazine pictures of people doing different kinds of work under the initial letters of those occupations.

Introduce a study of careers by pointing to the letters of the alphabet on the bulletin board. Each letter should promote some discussion on the different careers under it, so it will take several days to complete the discussion. Go as fast or as slowly as the children's interest seems to indicate.

Possibilities for interesting and varied pictures might be: *A*, actor, athlete, auto mechanic, auctioneer; *B*, barber, baker; *C*, carpenter, congressperson, construction worker; *D*, doctor, dairy farmer, designer; *E*, editor, electrician, engineer; *F*, commercial fisher, fire fighter, factory worker; *G*, governor, gardener; *H*, helicopter pilot, homemaker, hockey player; *I*, insurance agent, immigration officer, interpreter; *J*, judge, journalist, jockey; *K*, kennel operator, keypunch operator, key maker; *L*, lion tamer, logger; *M*, model, miner, minister; *N*, nurse, newscaster; *O*, orange grower, office worker; *P*, police officer, principal, pharmacist; *Q*, quilt maker, quarrier, quizmaster, quality-control engineer; *R*, rancher, real-estate agent; *S*, secretary, singer; *T*, teacher, telephone operator, travel agent, tumbler; *U*, union organizer, undertaker, umpire; *V*, violinist, vacuum-cleaner salesperson, veterinarian; *W*, writer, waiter, water-safety instructor; *X*, x-ray technician, xylophone player; *Y*, yeoman, yardman, yoga instructor; and *Z*, zoo-keeper, zither player.

III

Building Motor Skills

In recent years teachers have recognized the need to help children develop their motor skills, as immaturity in this area can cause the children difficulty in learning to read. In the past many teachers depended on carry-over from other readiness activities and on recess and after-school play to meet a child's need for motor-skill development. Today teachers feel these are not enough, so they are introducing more and more planned activities that can be used to foster such development in the classroom as well as on the playground.

The ideas and activities in this chapter range from simple, everyday games to more intensive ideas and approaches. All of these activities have proved to be enjoyable to children, as well as being specifically beneficial to the development of the children's motor skills.

82

Can You Find Your Chin?

OBJECTIVES developing memory, vocabulary, and language skills, and conceptualizing parts of the body.

MATERIALS none.

Sit in a circle with the children. Ask several "can you find . . ." questions. Ask the children to put a hand on the part of the body you mention. Whenever the children have difficulty finding one, or when they do not know what you mean, stop and explain that you are using the formal name for it, and show them which part you mean. For example, most children cannot find their navels, but they can easily put their fingers on their belly buttons.

Several questions you might ask are: "Can you find your knee?" "Can you find your eyelash?" "Can you find your elbow?" "Can you find your backbone (spine)?" "Can you find your calf?" "Can you find your index finger?" "Can you find your wrist?" "Can you find your eyelid?" "Can you find your nostril?" "Can you find your earlobe?" "Can you find your ankle?" "Can you find your lip?" "Can you find your fingernail?" "Can you find your heart?" "Can you find your throat?"

Continue playing the game at different times, until children become familiar with the proper names for the parts of their bodies.

83

John Brown's Body

OBJECTIVES conceptualizing the parts of the body and developing language.

MATERIALS butcher paper about four feet long, scissors, crayons or paint, cardboard for backing the pieces of the puzzle, and glue.

To make a John Brown puzzle, trace around a child who is lying on a sheet of butcher paper, to make a large silhouette of a body. Paint

it, or let the children color the figure. Paste or glue it to cardboard or tagboard. Then cut off the separate parts of the body, as in the illustration.

Sit in a large circle with the children. Stack the parts of the puzzle on your lap or on a nearby table or chair seat. Next, choose a child to select a part of the puzzle from the pile with his or her eyes shut. The child then looks at the piece and places it in the middle of the circle, saying, "This is John Brown's leg (body, head, arm, or whatever)."

That child then chooses another child to select another piece of the puzzle, with eyes shut. The second child will place the part in approximately its correct position in relationship to the first part, saying, "This is John Brown's body. It goes here." The second child chooses a third, and the game goes on.

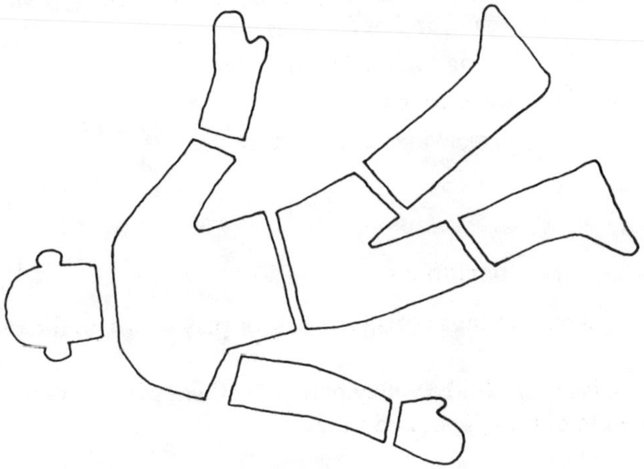

84

Follow-the-Leader Exercises

OBJECTIVE developing large muscles.

MATERIALS varied.

Begin having a short period of exercise each day. At first, lead the exercises yourself, to give the children an idea of what to do. Later, you can choose one child to be the leader for a day. Remind them that whatever the leader does, they must do also.

Select the leader for the next day at the end of each day's exercises, so that child can be thinking about what exercises he or she wants to use. You might encourage children to ask their parents to help them think of new exercises to show the class.

Some exercises children enjoy are:

- touching toes
- stretching to the ceiling
- running in place
- lying on the floor and "bicycling" in the air
- bending from the waist, each side, to the front, and to the back
- rolling the head on the neck
- clutching hands (making a fist, opening it, making a fist again, and opening it)
- swinging legs (alternately)
- knee bends
- arm swings and wrist twists

variations

Exercise to music. Use records, or play songs on the piano.

Give each child a volley ball, or let them pretend they each have a ball to bounce, toss, and catch.

Give each child a sheet of newspaper to move through the air, just as the leader moves his or her paper.

Have a dance session. Play a record and let the children dance anyway they feel. They may imitate parents or older brothers and sisters or just move to the music.

Give each child a jump rope or use one long rope and plan a jumping session.

Using the balance beam, ask the children to try several exercises in turn (jumping over, tiptoeing across, giant stepping across, and such).

85
Let's Pretend

OBJECTIVE developing large muscles.

MATERIALS none.

Have children stand where they can move freely without bumping into someone else. Give a series of "Let's Pretend" instructions something like the following.

Let's pretend:

"You are rabbits. Can you hop like a rabbit?"

"You are circus performers. Can you walk on a high wire?"

"You are jack-in-the-boxes. You are squeezed down tight in your box. Now someone opens the lid. You jump out!"

"You are elephants. Can you walk around like an elephant?"

"You are giraffes. Can you stretch your neck way up high to get the leaf at the top of the tree?"

"You are tiny seeds planted in the ground. You are growing taller and taller and taller."

"You are balloons. Someone blows you up fatter and fatter. They let you go. You float this way and that way. Now you hit a sharp branch. You have a hole in you. The air is going out of you faster and faster and faster, and you fall down on the ground, limp as can be."

86

Stringy, Stringy Puppets

OBJECTIVES developing large muscles and following directions.

MATERIALS none.

To develop large muscles, teach the poem "Stringy, Stringy Puppets," and have the children carry out the actions described below each line here.

See! I'm a stringy, stringy puppet.
Point to self, and slump.

My arms go flippity-flop.
Dangle your arms.

My legs go cloppity-clop.
Shake your legs loosely.

My head rolls round and round.
Dangle your head, and roll it around.

Like a floppity, moppity clown.
Continue to roll your head.

But when my strings are pulled
Stiffen your arms, legs, and head.

I stand up straight and tall.
Stand straight and tall.

Then my head and arms behave.
Point to your head, and then hold out your arms.

They never flop at all.
Shake your head "no."

87

Making Contact

OBJECTIVE developing large muscles.

MATERIALS three or four tagboard circles (6″ diameter), string or wire to hang them with, and decorative paper if desired.

Make some circles of tagboard, and hang them from the ceiling or from a wall. The circles can be covered with colorful contact paper or construction paper. Balloons will also serve, instead.

Hang the circles or balloons just out of reach of the children. Make some higher and some lower, to adjust for the different heights of the children.

Have as many children as there are circles try to make contact with the circles above them. Count to three slowly as the children stretch. On the count of three the children must return their hands to their sides.

Another group of children can then try to reach the circles. This can be repeated until all the children have had turns.

88

Walking the Wall

OBJECTIVE developing large muscles.

MATERIALS two sheets of butcher paper 3′ or 4′ long, masking tape, and felt pen.

Trace a path of four or five alternating left and right adult-size handprints on each of two sheets of butcher paper. Attach the sheets vertically to a wall about a foot apart, very securely. Divide the children into three teams. One team watches while the other two teams play the first game. Then the third team plays the winner, and the losing team watches. The playing teams line up relay-fashion with the nearest player about three feet from the butcher-paper paths.

On a signal from you, the first child on each team runs to the wall and, placing his or her hands on the handprints, "walks" up the paper and down again. (The others may help their teammates by counting, "UP, one, two, three, four, five, DOWN, six, seven, eight, nine.")

When the child is "down" again, he or she runs back to the team, tags the next player, and goes to the end of the line. The second player runs to the wall and repeats the process, and so forth.

The first team to finish walking the wall (when the final player runs back from the wall and tags the first player), is the winner.

89

Walking the Floor

OBJECTIVE developing large muscles.

MATERIALS construction-paper footprints (five per team).

Tape a series of construction-paper footprints on the floor, one for each team. Play in relay fashion, using the same rules as for "Walking the Wall" (Activity 88).

90

variation

Quickies

Use chalk or masking tape to indicate footprints or handprints. Make circles, squares, or *x*s for the prints. You could even use a chalkboard for "Walking the Wall."

91

Can You Imagine?

OBJECTIVE developing small muscles.

MATERIALS one sheet of drawing paper for each child and crayons.

Give each child a sheet of manila drawing paper and a crayon. Ask all the children to put on their thinking caps because today they will be playing a game with their imaginations.

When all are ready, ask the children to imagine they are going to visit a pretzel-stick factory: "See the big pretzel-making machine.

Look at the way it makes all those nice, even pretzel sticks. See how the bags are being filled."

Ask that each child draw a bag on the paper and then fill the bag with pretzel sticks. When they have finished, continue with the imagination game. Say, "Oops, look at the pretzel machine. It has a problem. It's gone on the blink. It won't shut off. Oh, goodness! Pretzels are going everywhere. Your pretzel bag is overflowing. Make pretzel sticks all over your paper!"

The children will enjoy making as many pretzel sticks as they can on their papers. When their papers are almost full, explain that the repairman finally arrived and fixed the machine. Now they can stop making pretzels on their papers.

variation

They can use the other sides of the papers for an imaginary story about a broken donut machine.

92

Run, Tillie, Run!

OBJECTIVES developing large muscles and conceptualizing parts of the body.

MATERIALS two chairs for each team.

Divide the class into three or four relay teams having approximately six children to a team. Each team stands behind a home plate (chair #1) and runs around an outfield goal (chair #2). The chairs should be ten or twelve feet apart.

Each team lines up in a row behind its home plate. Explain the game by saying, "I will tell you which part of your body to hold. Keep your hand on that part of your body while you run. When I say, 'Run, Tillie, Run!' run to your outfield chair, go around it, and run back to home plate. When the first player touches home plate, the second player starts, and the first person goes to the end of the line and sits down. The team whose members all finish first will be the winner. While you run, remember to keep your hand on the part of your body that I've mentioned, and remember to sit down at the end of the line when you have finished your run."

Some sample directions would be: Tillie, hold your head; Tillie, hold your ankle; . . . your knee; . . . your wrist.

93

Watch Out for the Wolf!

OBJECTIVE developing large muscles.

MATERIALS a tree, a pole, or a wall to represent the wolf's home.

This is an exciting activity to use after telling the story "The Three Little Pigs." It can be played inside or outside.

Choose one child to be the wolf. The wolf stands facing a wall or a tree with his back to all the other children. He pretends to sleep.

The other children are pigs. When the teacher says GO, they start from a starting line (about ten or twelve feet from the wolf) and try to creep up on the wolf without being seen. The wolf counts to ten, wakes up, and shouts "FREEZE!" The pigs must stop and be very still. Anyone the wolf sees moving has to go back to the starting line. The pig to reach the wolf first becomes the next wolf.

94

Jump, Jack, Jump!

OBJECTIVES developing large muscles and language.

MATERIALS a candle or a soup can (or other object that size to represent the candlestick).

Place a candle or something to represent a candlestick in the middle of the circle. Teach the children the rhyme "Jack Be Nimble."

Jack, be nimble.
Jack, be quick.
Jack, jump over the candlestick.
Jack jumped high,
Jack jumped low,
Jack jumped over and burned his toes.

Next, tell the children that you know a game that goes with the poem. Choose someone to be Jack. Then, have all the other children say the poem. Jack jumps over the candlestick, high and low. (Jack jumps from a standing position.)

After the children say the last line, ask, "Did Jack burn his toes?" Everyone answers "no" if Jack was successful and "yes" if Jack was not.

Choose another Jack, and continue playing as long as you wish.

95

Pathfinding

OBJECTIVE developing small muscles.

MATERIALS scissors and duplicated patterns (a week's supply per child).

Cutting paper is an excellent way to develop small muscles. Any number of activities will give cutting practice, but sometimes it is good to follow a specific plan for cutting. The simple exercise plan here is intended to last one week.

Beforehand, duplicate five easy-to-cut patterns similar to those shown here.

Each day that week, give the children a page to cut and a pair of scissors. Demonstrate the way you want that day's pattern cut. You might say that this is a pathfinding game. Ask them to cut right down the path, being very careful not to let their scissors stray out into the bushes.

This activity could well follow the introduction of scissors as a classroom tool. The practice of cleaning up after themselves can also be reinforced each day.

variation

Throwaway Basketball

Place wastebaskets in appropriate spots, and ask the children to wad their practice papers into balls and toss them into the nearest wastebaskets. This is fun, and it continues the small-muscle development.

variation

Cutting Folders

Use large sheets of 12″ x 18″ newsprint or construction paper to make a folder for each child. Print their names on their folders with felt pen. Attach the folders to a bulletin board with thumbtacks, or let the children keep their folders in their personal cupboards or shelves. Each day, have them add their cutting exercises to their folders.

They can also be encouraged to add other things they've cut, such as pictures from magazines or catalogs. They can take the folders home at the end of the week. You could attach a short note, like the one here, to explain the activity.

Dear Parents:

This week we have been working on some special exercises to help in the development of the small muscles. Cutting is one way to develop and strengthen those muscles, and it also gives practice in eye-hand coordination. This is an important first step in learning to write.

You may wish your children to continue cutting at home. Please remind them that they have been taught to use scissors properly and to clean up after themselves.

Sincerely,

96

Cut-and-Paste Shapes

OBJECTIVES developing small muscles and language, and recognizing numbers.

MATERIALS one sheet 9″ x 12″ drawing paper per child, scraps of construction paper, scissors for each child, and paste.

Give each child a sheet of 9″ x 12″ drawing paper with his or her name on it. Have a supply of multicolored construction-paper scraps on hand, or allow the children to use your scrap box. Encourage them each to select three colors they feel go well together. Then, have them cut the scraps they have chosen into shapes of their choice. Next, have them paste the shapes onto their drawing papers in pleasing arrangements.

97

variation

Introducing a Number

Before starting the project, introduce a number—3, for example. Offer the children many opportunities during the session to count threes (fingers, girls, boys, chairs, colors, scraps). Remind them of the story of "The Three Bears" or the "Three Little Pigs." You might even tell these stories if time permits. Demonstrate how to write the number, and then explain the cutting project. When they have finished, print or have the children print the numeral *3* on their papers.

98

variation

Recognizing Numbers

Have them number each shape with crayon or felt pen.

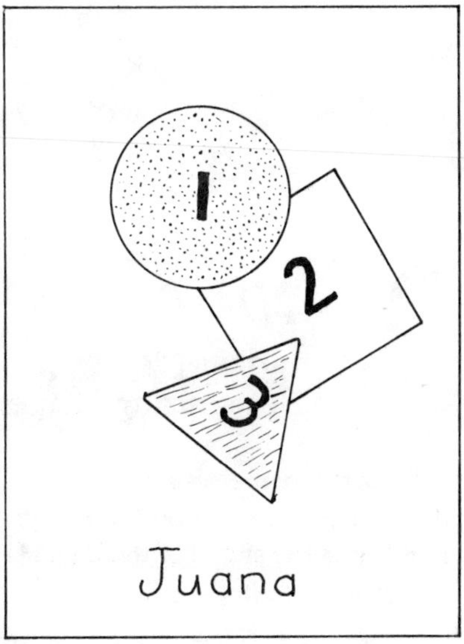

99

variation
Number Reinforcement

Print the name of the same number on each paper before the children begin. Ask the children to look at the number, read it, and then cut that many shapes to paste onto their papers.

100

variation
Color Reinforcement

Give each child a sheet of drawing paper with the name of a color printed at the top. Explain that they are to cut and paste only scraps of that color. You could place old magazines and catalogs for them to cut near the scrap box to add variety to the selection of shades.

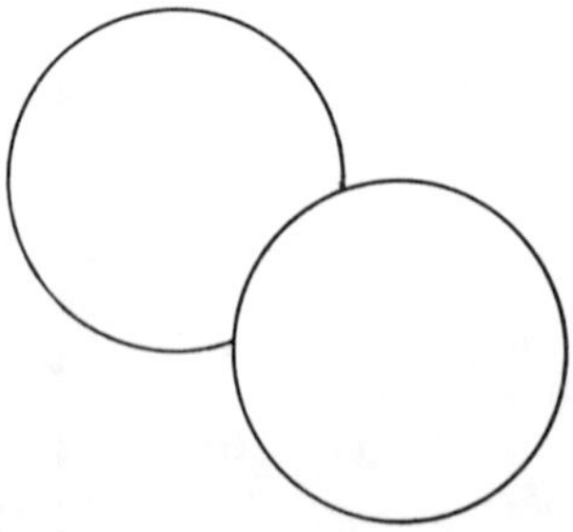

101

variation
Recognizing Shapes

Print the name of a geometric shape at the top of each sheet of drawing paper or draw the shape at the top with felt pen. Explain that this is the shape of the day. Have them cut and paste that shape only.

102

Color-Cut-and-Paste Clowns

OBJECTIVES developing small muscles and independence.

MATERIALS scissors, paste, crayons, and duplicated patterns.

As children learn how to listen and follow directions, they become ready to develop greater independence. Color-cut-and-paste clowns is an independent activity that works nicely as part of a unit on the circus or as a decorating activity for a school carnival.

Duplicate patterns ($8\frac{1}{2}'' \times 11''$), similar to the one shown here. Tell the children they are patterns for making cutout clowns. Give general directions to color all of the parts first, making a design on the clown's suit, and such, and then to cut out the pieces and paste them together. Make a finished clown yourself ahead of time to show how the project looks when it is completed. Then explain that this is a project they can do all by themselves.

Some younger children may require help with cutting, but encourage them to do as much as they can before they ask you for help.

variation

Prepare a set of $8\frac{1}{2}''$ x $11''$ duplicated sheets, as shown. Give children one of each, and mention that you have a few extras in case someone misplaces a part. This version of the project involves more parts to keep track of, but the results are most effective, and more mature students find it more challenging than making the smaller clowns.

103

Drop It, Sock It Games

OBJECTIVES developing large muscles and eye-hand coordination, and reinforcing numbers.

MATERIALS varied.

For motor development, play "Drop It, Sock It" games in which the children work for a class score. Five good ones are listed here:

1. Each one drops a clothespin in a bottle or a cardboard container. If they sock it in, they win one point for the class.
2. The children toss wads of paper into a wastebasket a few feet away. Sock it in, and they get another point for the class score.
3. They drop cotton balls into a container.
4. They drop poker chips onto a paper bull's eye.
5. Outdoor versions could include dropping rocks into a container or balls through hula hoops.

Play one or more "Drop It, Sock It" games a day, and keep a record of the total class points for the day. Each day the class can try to get a higher score.

104

Hula Hoop Puddles

OBJECTIVES developing language and large muscles.

MATERIALS three or four hula hoops and chalk or masking tape.

Place three or four hula hoops around the room on the floor. Pretend they are puddles. Encourage the children to make up stories about why they are splashing and jumping in the puddles, such as: "I am a duck. I splash in puddles." "I am a person trying to get home in a rainstorm." Or, "I'm an elephant looking for a shelter from the rain."

105

variation

Acting Poems

Read one of the many rainy-day poems found in most books of children's poems, such as "Pitter Patter" by Dorothy W. Baruch, in the *Read-to-Me Storybook* compiled by the Child Study Association (New York: Crowell, 1947).

Have the children act out parts of the poem. In "Pitter Patter" the children could be trucks going rumbledy rumble, rumbledy rumble through the puddles; airplanes going brrum, brrum-ummmmm; cows going moo-moo-moooo; ducks going quack, quack; sailboats going flap, flap; trains going puff chuff, puff chuff and whoo, whoo whoo; and a car going slippery slish.

106

variation

Down the Drain

Play "Down the Drain" by placing the hula hoops around a six-inch chalk circle. Have one child stand in each hoop. When you say *go*, the children try to push the hula hoops to the drain, using only their feet.

107

Make a Batch of Finger Paint

OBJECTIVES developing large muscles and reinforcing measuring.

MATERIALS 1 quart saucepan, $\frac{1}{2}$ cup liquid starch, $1\frac{1}{2}$ cups boiling water, $\frac{1}{2}$ cup soap flakes, 1 tablespoon glycerin (optional), and food coloring.

Finger painting is a good way for children to develop motor skills. The activity can be made more interesting if the children help make their own finger paint. This also reinforces concepts of measuring.

RECIPE FOR FINGER PAINT

Mix $\frac{1}{2}$ cup starch with enough cold water to make a smooth paste. Add $1\frac{1}{2}$ cups boiling water, and cook until glossy. Stir in $\frac{1}{2}$ cup *soap flakes* (not soap powder) while mixture is warm. For extra smoothness add 1 tbsp glycerin when the mixture is cool. Add food coloring. (This is enough to give twenty or thirty children a modest amount to work with.)

108

Dough Time in No Time

OBJECTIVES developing small muscles, solving problems, and measuring.

MATERIALS large mixing bowl, 2 cups flour, 1 cup salt, 2 tablespoons cooking oil, water, and food coloring.

Learning to measure is almost a side benefit when children become involved in making their own "Play-doh." The recipe is easy, and the dough keeps in a tightly covered coffee can about two weeks.

After you introduce and discuss measuring cups and spoons, print the recipe on the chalkboard or on a sheet of paper tacked above the worktable. Begin by asking one child to measure the first cup of flour. Then ask another to measure the second cup. Continue in this way, letting as many children as possible measure things. All the children should have an opportunity to squeeze the dough when it's ready.

Then divide the finished product among them and let them experiment with making their own creations. If there is not enough dough to go around, discuss the problem, and decide how to solve it. (Make another batch.)

FUN DOUGH

Mix together in a large bowl: 2 cups flour, 1 cup salt, 2 tbsp cooking oil. Wet with water. (Experiment until it feels right.) Add a squirt of food coloring. Squeeze or knead until the dough feels right for modeling (like commercial modeling clay).

109

Pudding Painting

OBJECTIVES developing small muscles and sensory perception.

MATERIALS two or three boxes instant pudding (one box for 8 or 10 children), milk, dishes, and a sheet of fingerpainting paper per child.

For muscle development, introduce a fun and tasty kind of finger paint. Mix a batch of instant pudding. Give each child a small dish (margarine or pot pie containers are excellent) of pudding and a large sheet of finger-painting paper. Demonstrate how to dip the fingers into the pudding and paint a pudding picture. Let the children's pictures dry before they take them home. Clean-up is seldom a problem.

You can introduce this activity by explaining that artists do not always use paint or marble. Sometimes they use other materials that seem a little strange. For example, some work with old junk, metal scraps, straw, yarn, sand, clay, and stone. Remind them of examples they may have seen locally. Tell them artists often experiment with different materials. Sometimes the experiments work, and sometimes they don't. Today, they will be experimenting with a new painting material, too. Today they will try painting with pudding, and when they are finished, they may decide whether they like this way of painting or not.

You might also use this activity to reinforce a lesson on the senses. Taste, touch, sight, and smell all come into play.

110

Catch-a-Carton

OBJECTIVES developing muscles and eye-hand coordination.

MATERIALS a 12″ ruler or a straight stick about that length (one for each child), a half-pint milk carton with top cut off to make an open box, and a piece of string about 14 inches long (one of each per child), and scissors.

This is best for classes in which most children can tie knots. Begin by discussing toys: "Where do you buy toys?Do you like shopping for them? What could you do if there were no stores that sold toys? Do you suppose you could make a toy?"

Continue by telling the children that long ago there were no toy stores in many towns. Children, with the help of their parents, did, indeed, have to make their own toys and games. They used materials they found around home.

Explain that today they will be making a game using things they find in the schoolroom. Pass out a ruler, a cut-off milk carton, and a string to each.

Ask them to tie one end of the string to the ruler or stick. (Use sticks if you plan to let the children take the project home with them.) The string should be tied about a third of the way from one end of the stick. Have the children punch a small hole in the center of the bottom of each milk carton using scissors or pencils. Next have them put the string through the hole from outside the box and tie a knot in the end of the string that is inside the carton.

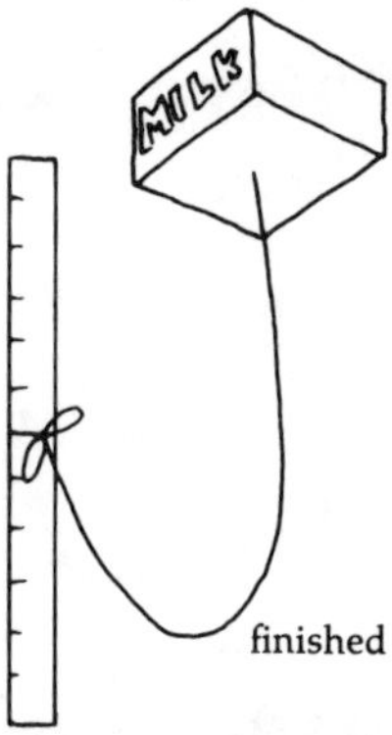

finished toy

To play the game, they hold the long ends of the rulers in one hand and swing the cartons up into the air. The object is to try to catch the cartons on the ends of the rulers.

111
Funny People

OBJECTIVES developing small muscles and reinforcing knowledge of the body.

MATERIALS old magazines, scissors and glue and a piece of light-colored construction paper for each child.

Discuss the body—a person has one head, one body, two arms, two legs, two feet, and so forth. Give each child a sheet of construction paper. Ask the class to look through the magazines and each cut out a head from one person and other parts of the body from other pictures. Have them arrange the parts on their papers and glue them in place.

Display the delightful results on a "Funny People" bulletin board.

IV

Special Days and Special Seasons

This chapter includes more activities that help develop the skills we have dealt with previously. But these activities are keyed to special times in the school year. Among them are several ideas for gifts the children can make to take home on special occasions.

Halloween

112
Strange Visitor

OBJECTIVES developing language and listening.

MATERIALS flannel for parts of the visitor (head, 4″ x 4″; shoulders, 2″ x 4″; arms, 3″ x 1″; body, 4″ x 4″; waist, 2″ x 2″; legs, 2″ x 2″; hands, 1″ x 3″; feet, 1″ x 3″).

Sometime before Halloween, turn the old Scottish folktale "Strange Visitor" into a delightful flannel-board story. Besides being fun, it helps children develop language and listening skills.

Read the story (below), placing the individual parts of the man on the flannel board when they first are mentioned. Stop at the first refrain, and help the children learn to repeat it. Demonstrate the action. Then continue with the story, helping the children with each refrain if necessary.

STRANGE VISITOR

There once was an old, old lady who lived all alone in the woods, and she wanted someone to come and visit her, and while she waited, she spun cloth.

And still she sat, *fold hands in lap*
And still she spun, *roll hands*
And still she waited for someone to come.

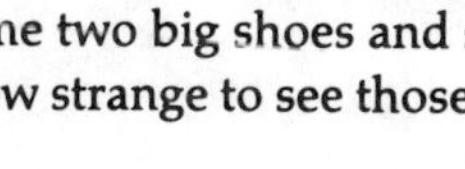

Then one dark, dark night when the old lady was sitting spinning, she heard a sound at the door. She said, "Come in." Then, squ-e-e-k went the door, and in came two big shoes and sat themselves down, and she thought, "Oh, how strange to see those big, big shoes on the cold, cold floor, but . . .

Repeat refrain.

Soon she heard another sound and she said, "Come in." Then squ-e-e-k went the door and in came two short, short legs and sat themselves down on the big, big shoes on the cold, cold floor, but . . .

Repeat refrain.

Before very long she heard another sound outside, and she said, "Come in." Then squ-e-e-k went the door, and in came a wee, wee waist and sat on the short, short legs on those big, big shoes on the cold, cold floor, but . . .

Repeat refrain.

And while she was looking, she heard another knock, and said, "Come in." Then squ-e-e-k went the door, and in flew two broad, broad shoulders and sat themselves down on the wee, wee waist, and

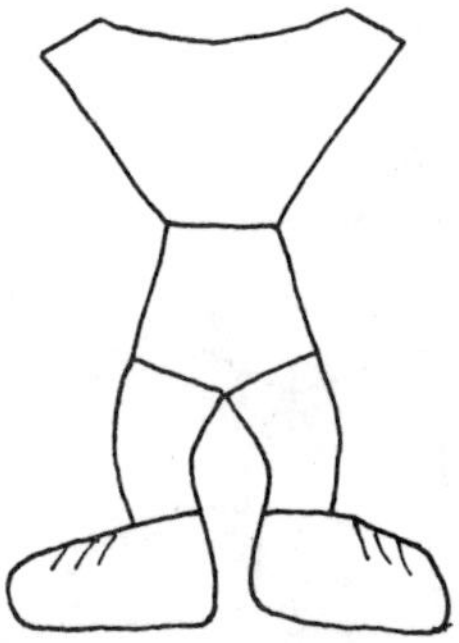

the old lady thought, "Oh, how strange to see those broad, broad shoulders on the wee, wee waist on the short, short legs in those big, big shoes on the cold, cold floor." But . . .

Repeat refrain.

And as she was spinning, she heard another sound, so she said, "Come in." Squ-e-e-k went the door, and in jumped two long, long arms and hung themselves on the broad, broad shoulders, and she thought, "Oh, how strange to see those long, long arms on the broad, broad shoulders, on that wee, wee waist, on those short, short legs, on those big, big shoes, on that cold, cold floor." But . . .

Repeat refrain.

And in just a few minutes she heard another sound, so she said, "Come in." Squ-e-e-k went the door, and in came two fat hands and fastened themselves onto those long, long arms, and she thought, "Oh, how strange to see those fat, fat hands on those long, long arms, on those broad, broad shoulders, on that wee, wee waist, on those short, short legs, on those big, big feet, on that cold, cold floor." But . . .

Repeat refrain.

In a few more minutes she heard another sound at the door, so she said, "Come in." Squ-e-e-k went the door, and in came a round, round pumpkin head and plopped itself right on top of the broad, broad shoulders, on that wee, wee waist, on those short, short legs, on those big, big feet, on that cold, cold floor.

Then the old woman said, "Oh, how strange to see that round, round head on those broad, broad shoulders with the long, long arms and the fat, fat hands, on the wee, wee waist, on those short, short legs on the big, big feet, on the cold, cold floor."

So she said: "Where did you get such big, big feet?"

And someone said, "Much walking, much walking."

And she said, "Well, where did you get such short, short legs?"

And someone said, "Much running, much running."

And she asked, "Where did you get such broad, broad shoulders?"

And someone said, "Carrying brooms, carrying brooms."

Then she asked, Where did you get such long, long arms?"

And someone said, "Swinging an axe, swinging an axe."

And then she asked, "Where did you get such fat, fat hands?"

And someone said, "Threshing wheat, threshing wheat."

Then she said, "Well, where did you get such a round, round head, and what did you come for?"

And someone said . . . "YOU ! ! !"

And that is the story of the man with the round, round head and the fat, fat hands, on the long, long arms, on those broad, broad shoulders, on that wee, wee waist, on those short, short legs, in those big, big shoes, on the COLD, COLD FLOOR!

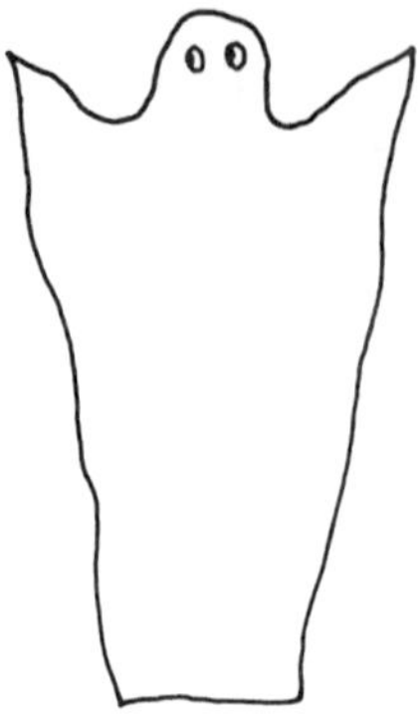

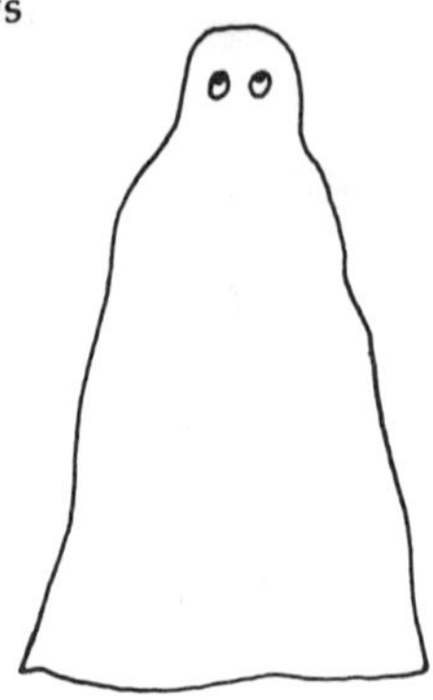

113

Tracing Ghosts

OBJECTIVES developing visual perception, vocabulary, eye-hand coordination, and math concepts.

MATERIALS five or six tagboard ghost patterns, and a 9″ x 12″ sheet of drawing paper, scissors, and a black crayon for each child.

Make five or six ghost shapes from tagboard for patterns. Give each child a sheet of 9″ x 12″ white drawing paper and a pencil. Let the children take turns using the patterns. Explain that when they finish tracing, they can cut out their ghosts and then use black crayon to make a pair of very scary eyes on them.

This presents an opportunity to introduce the term *pair*: "What does it mean? Your eyes come in pairs. Do any other parts of your body come in pairs?" And so on.

114

Gone with the Ghost

OBJECTIVES developing memory and visual perception, reinforcing geometric shapes.

MATERIALS none.

Reinforce the concept of circle by asking the children to sit in a pumpkin circle. Choose a child to be the ghost. While the others

close their eyes, the ghost silently takes a child from the circle and leads that child to a prearranged hiding place everyone knows about.

The ghost then makes a ghostly sound to signal the others to open their eyes and guess which child has been taken. If they guess correctly, the ghost must return the child to the pumpkin circle. If the children cannot guess, the ghost keeps the child, and the game continues.

Encourage the children to observe the circle carefully when their eyes are open so they will be able to guess who is missing and thus get them back from the ghost.

The ghost could also take more than one child at a time. Or a new ghost could be chosen for each turn.

115

Triangle Witches

OBJECTIVES developing visual perception and reinforcing recognition of triangles.

MATERIALS one 9" x 12" sheet of orange construction paper for each child, crayons, paste, black construction-paper triangles.

Introduce or reinforce the children's recognition of the triangle shape by having them make triangle witches for Halloween. In advance, cut enough large equilateral triangles so each child will have one for a witch body. Cut medium triangles for hats and two very small triangles each for shoes. Distribute these pieces along with 9" x 12" sheets of orange construction paper for a background.

Show the children a sample witch you have made with your triangles. Explain that the best way to start is by pasting the large triangle in the center of the paper. This is the witch's body. Next draw a head, two arms, and two legs on the body. Put the medium-size triangle on the head for a hat. The little triangles are shoes. Paste them on the witch's feet.

116
Creative Halloween Masks

OBJECTIVE developing creative thinking.

MATERIALS a large grocery sack for each child, scraps of construction paper, scissors, crayons, and paste.

Children will enjoy making creative Halloween masks, even though they may wear other costumes on the day of your party.

Ahead of time, cut off the side sections of the sack about halfway up. This allows the sack to fit easily over the child's head and shoulders. Then fit a sack over each child's head, in turn, to get the approximate position of the child's eyes, and cut two large eyeholes. The child can begin right away to decorate the mask with crayons, paper hair, eyelashes, a collar, or whatever.

Thanksgiving

117

Thanksgiving Cut and Color

OBJECTIVES building vocabulary, learning history, and developing small muscles.

MATERIALS duplicated sheets of Indian babies, crayons, scissors, stapler, and brown construction paper (sheets 9″ x 12″ and strips $1\frac{1}{2}$″ x 18″).

Duplicate a pattern of an Indian baby. (The pattern should pretty well fill a sheet of $8\frac{1}{2}$″ x 11″ ditto paper.) The illustration, while not an infant, does provide an interesting picture for children to color and it can stimulate further conversation on how little babies might have been dressed.

Many teachers prefer to make the papooses in advance. This saves time, but the children may be allowed to help if the project does not seem too difficult for the age and the development of the particular group. I recommend that a teacher make a sample first and then decide whether class participation is desirable.

First staple two sheets of 9″ x 12″ brown construction paper together, one on top of the other. Round off the four corners as shown in the illustration.

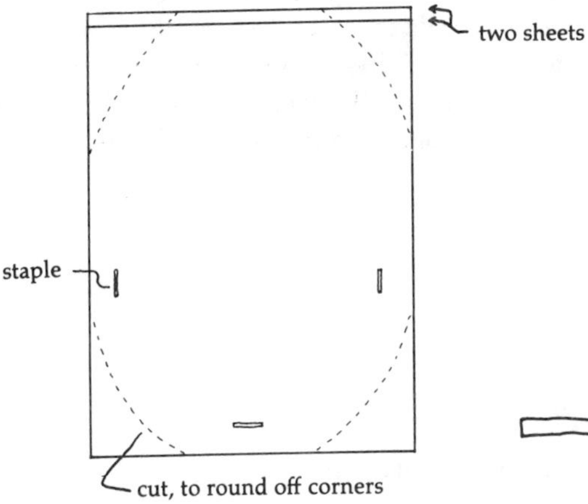

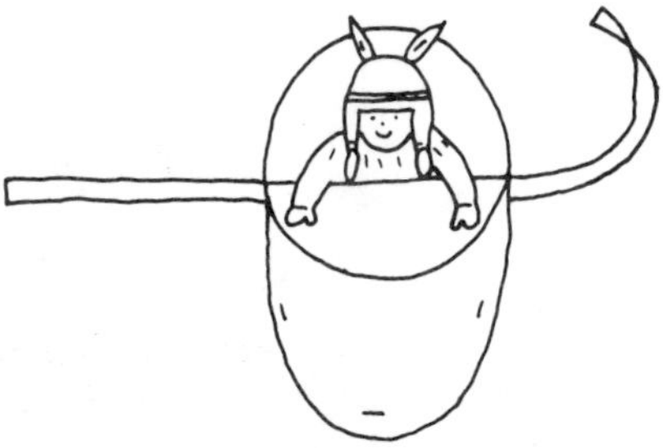

Fold the top of one section down about one quarter of the way. Insert one end of a construction-paper tie (about $1\frac{1}{2}$″ wide and 18″ long) on each side between the flap and the back section of paper. Staple through all three layers, making sure the ties are secure.

In November, before Thanksgiving, classes often discuss Native Americans. Young children enjoy hearing that mothers and fathers of some tribes would call their babies papooses. They also find it fascinating that a mother would carry her baby around on her back. Tell about the papooses, and encourage the children to try and think of why mothers might carry their children that way.

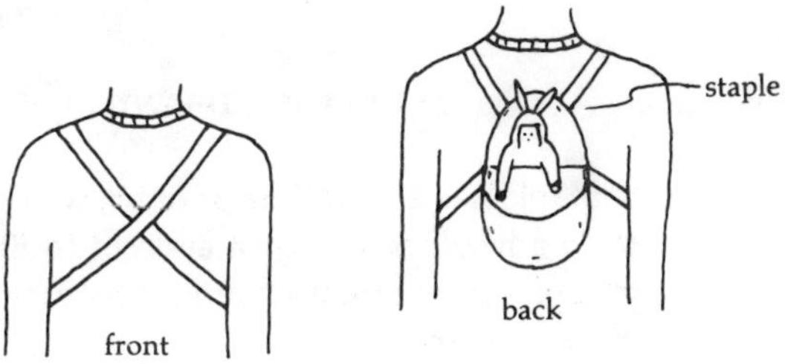

After the discussion, give each child a duplicated outline drawing of an Indian baby to color. Explain that when they have finished coloring the babies, they will cut them out and place them in a carrier like Indian papooses. Then, either give the children prepared carriers or give them the materials to make them by themselves.

When they are done, the children can wear the papooses. Staple the other ends of the ties across the back and over the shoulders. Provide a mirror so they can see themselves wearing their papooses.

118

Thanksgiving Drama

OBJECTIVES developing language, creative thinking, and art, and learning history.

MATERIALS construction paper (brown for Indian headdresses, various colors for feathers, black for boy's Pilgrim hats, yellow for buckles, white for girl's Pilgrim hats), scissors, stapler, and paste.

Tell the story of the first Thanksgiving, or read *The Thanksgiving Story* by Alice Dalgliesh (New York: Scribner's, 1954). Then discuss with the children how they might reenact the first Thanksgiving in the classroom.

Plan a playlet together. Select some children to be Indians and others to be Pilgrims. Help each group make simple Pilgrim hats or Indian headbands to wear as costumes.

INDIAN HEADBANDS

Staple two 2″ x 18″ strips of brown construction paper together to form a headband. Adjust and cut to fit child's head. Make feather triangles from bright-colored construction paper, and staple them in place, as shown.

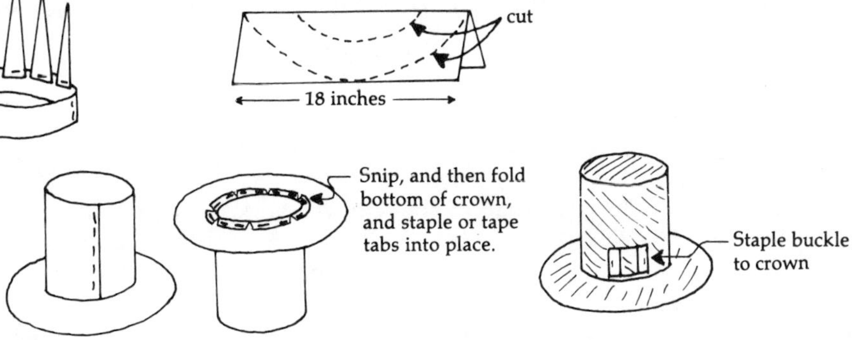

BOY'S PILGRIM HAT

Use a 12″ x 18″ sheet of construction paper. Fold in half the long way and cut out a semicircle for the brim, as illustrated. Make the crown by rolling a sheet of 9″ x 12″ construction paper to fit the center hole of the brim, and then staple or tape it to the brim. Add a yellow construction-paper buckle to the front, and the hat is complete.

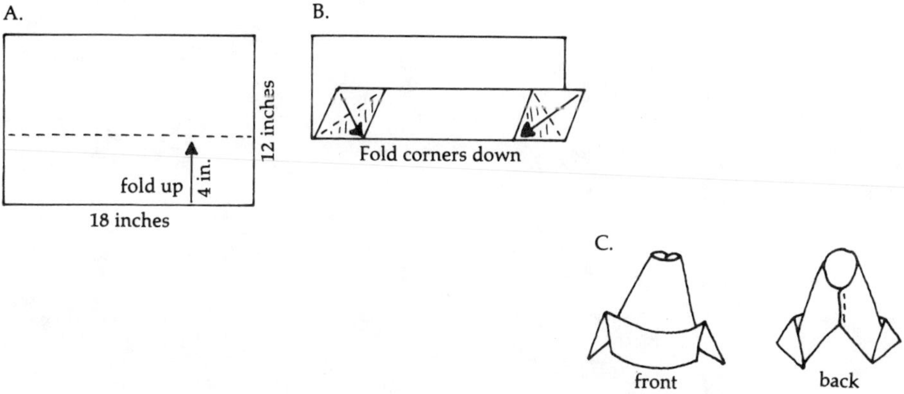

GIRL'S PILGRIM HAT

Use a sheet of white 12″ x 18″ construction paper. Make a fold the long way, a third of the way up. Fold the corners of this third back. Roll the hat to fit the child's head, and staple at the top.

119

Thanksgiving Gobble

OBJECTIVE developing large muscles.

MATERIALS none.

After you've talked about the foods eaten by the Pilgrims on their first Thanksgiving, it is fun to play the game "Thanksgiving Gobble," either outdoors or at one end of a room with the furniture moved aside.

Choose one child to be a Pilgrim. The rest are the turkeys. The turkeys stand in the forest at one end of the play area, which is marked off by a goal line as a safety area for turkeys. The Pilgrim starts out at the far end of the play area, pretending to scatter bread crumbs while gobbling like a turkey to fool the turkeys in the forest into thinking there are some turkeys in the clearing also. The gobbling turkeys are fooled, and they come slowly out of the forest to eat the crumbs. When the turkeys get close, the Pilgrim yells "THANKSGIVING!" And he tries to catch as many turkeys as he can. The turkeys try to run back to the forest. Those who are tagged become Pilgrims.

The game continues until all the turkeys have been caught.

Christmas and Hanukkah

120
Latkes for Hanukkah

OBJECTIVE socialization.

MATERIALS 2 eggs, 3 cups grated and drained potatoes, 4 tbsb grated onion, 1 tsp salt, $\frac{1}{4}$ tsp pepper, 2 tbsp cracker crumbs or matzo meal, frying pan, heating element, butter, utensils, plates, knives, forks, and jelly or applesauce.

Invite a Jewish parent or another resource person to visit the classroom and discuss the meaning of the celebration of Hanukkah on or around December 20. If possible, ask this person to help the children make and serve latkes, the delicious potato pancakes so often served during this celebration.

If most of the children are not Jewish, prepare them a day or two ahead for learning something about different religions and the different ways people believe. You might use the example of their own differences in appearance: "Some people are tall, others are short. You have blond hair, and Joey has black hair." "The ways people worship can also be different, and just as we respect differences in the way people look, we also respect differences in religions." Continue the discussion, encouraging the children to think of questions they might like to ask the resource person.

Also, prepare the guest for some of the questions children might ask, such as, "Do you believe in Santa Claus?" "Do you have a Christmas tree?" Or "Why do you eat latkes during Hanukkah?"

LATKES

In a large mixing bowl beat two eggs. Then add three cups grated and drained potatoes, four tablespoons grated onion, one teaspoon salt, a quarter teaspoon pepper, and two tablespoons cracker crumbs or matzo meal. Stir until well mixed. Heat a quarter cup fat or butter in a frying pan and drop the potato mixture into it by the tablespoonful. Fry until browned on both sides. Keep pancakes hot until all are fried. Add more fat or butter to the frying pan as needed. Serves 8.

Each child will need a plate, knife, and fork. Serve the pancakes with applesauce or jelly. This could be put over the pancakes or served on the edge of the plate and the pancakes dipped into it.

121

Christmas Chains

OBJECTIVES developing small muscles, and socialization.

MATERIALS many ½″ wide strips of colored construction paper 6 to 8 inches long, and paste.

As old as the idea may be, most children do enjoy making paper chains, and it is a good exercise for small-muscle development.

Give each child a supply of the narrow strips of paper. Demonstrate how to put the chain together by pasting the ends of one strip together to make the first circle and then sliding another strip of paper through that circle and then pasting its ends together, and so on. Explain that chains can be very long or very short, and that they can be used to decorate the classroom or to take home for their trees.

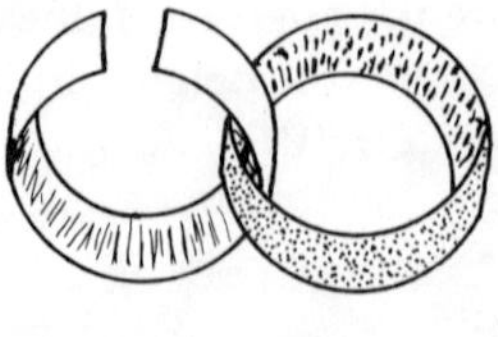

variation

Orange and black chains could be made for Halloween decorations.

122

A Christmas Bulletin Board

OBJECTIVES developing small muscles, and socialization.

MATERIALS green and red construction paper, crayons, sheets or scraps of Christmas wrapping paper, yarn, ribbons, scissors, a large cutout Christmas tree with a star on top.

Use red and green Christmas chains (Activity 121) as a border around a bulletin board and as decorations for a large construction-paper Christmas tree displayed there. Have the children make packages to put around the bottom of the tree by cutting rectangles from Christmas wrapping paper or construction paper. Yarn, ribbon, or commercially prepared bows could be attached to the tops of the "boxes."

For added interest, have the children draw small pictures of things they would like to get for Christmas. Cut them out, and staple them onto packages the children have made, so the packages serve as attractive frames for their pictures.

123

Tree Decoration

OBJECTIVES socialization, art, and developing eye-hand coordination.

MATERIALS one small Styrofoam ball for each child, toothpicks, gold or silver spray paint, and paper clips or pipe cleaners (one per ornament).

An easy-to-make tree decoration is always a nice gift for a child's parents. It can be kept year after year and the memories of a child's early years relived, Christmas after Christmas.

Give each child a Styrofoam ball and several toothpicks. Show them how to poke the toothpicks into the ball all over, letting some stick out farther than others. Open paper clips and stick one into each ball for a hanger. Spray with paint.

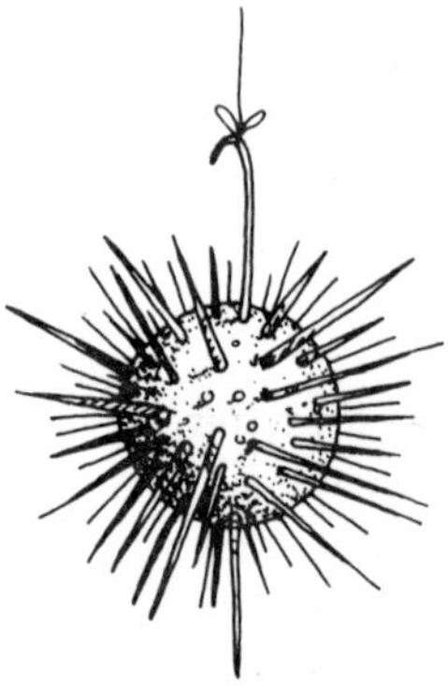

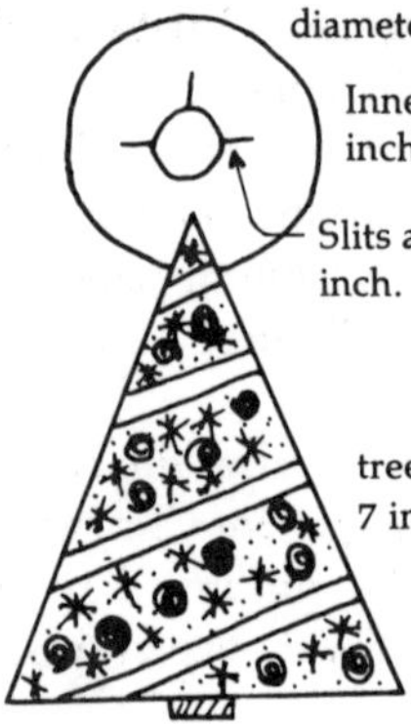

124

Doorknob Decorations

OBJECTIVES developing eye-hand coordination and making a gift for parents.

MATERIALS red felt (½ yard yields about twenty 4-inch circles); green felt (enough for a tree 7 inches tall for each child); glue; and a selection of star stickers, beads, sequins, and the like.

These attractive decorations that slip over the front doorknob, also can be saved year after year in the box of Christmas mementos.

Precut a circle from the red felt and a tree from green felt for each child. Staple the trees to the circles as shown.

The children decorate the trees by gluing small scraps of red felt to the green trees or by pasting stars on them. (It would be a good idea to make a sample ahead of time to show them.)

125

Decorated Soap

OBJECTIVES making a gift for parents, and art training.

MATERIALS a bar of soap for each child, glitter, old Christmas cards or wrapping paper, and white glue.

Show a sample to the class. Then have the children look through a supply of old Christmas cards and select pictures they like—one picture each. Remind them the pictures must be small enough to fit on a bar of soap. After they cut out their pictures, spread white glue thinly on top of their bars of soap. Have the children press the pictures in place and sprinkle the soap around them with glitter.

variation

If you don't use this idea at Christmas, you might for Mother's Day. The children can select pictures of flowers to paste on the soap. Or you might cut colored tissue paper into half-inch squares for the children to wad up and glue on the soap to look like flowers.

126

Christmas Stationery

OBJECTIVES making a gift for mother, and following directions.

MATERIALS six sheets of ditto or mimeograph paper and six envelopes per child, one sheet of 12″ x 18″ construction paper for each child, and at least six Christmas stickers per child.

Give each child six sheets of ditto paper and six envelopes. Show the children how to fold the paper in half the short way to make

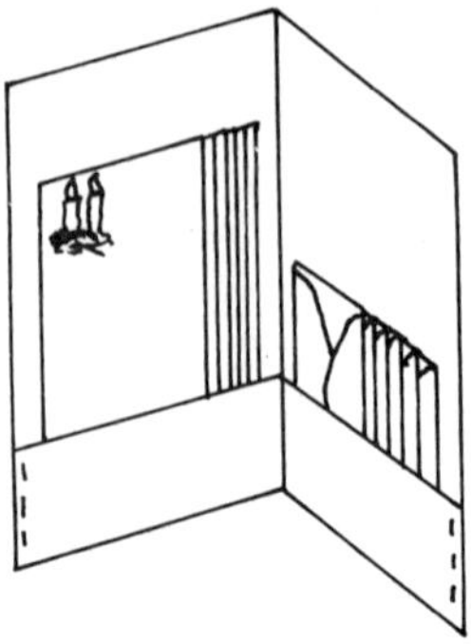

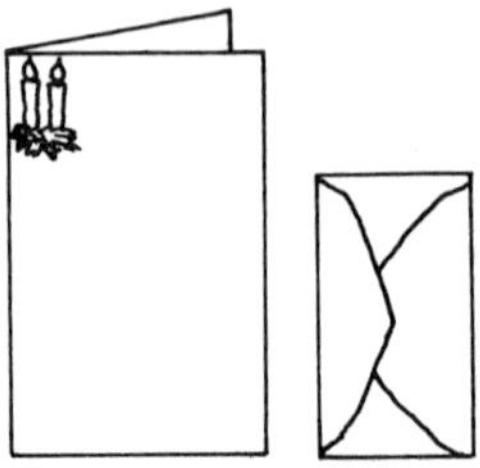

writing paper. Demonstrate how the paper should open. Explain how it will be used: "Mom will write letters on this special stationery, so you must remember not to stick the decoration in the middle of the paper. Put the sticker at the top so there will be room to write down here."

When the paper is folded correctly, give each child six stickers. Explain that one sticker goes at the top of each folded sheet of paper. Demonstrate.

Then use 12" x 18" sheets of construction paper for folders to hold the stationery. First have the children fold them across once the long way and staple as shown. Then have them fold in half the other way like a book. The children can then decorate the fronts of the folders and slip the envelopes in one side and the writing paper in the other.

variation

This would also make a nice Mother's Day gift if you do not use the idea at Christmas. For Mother's Day use flower stickers instead of Christmas stickers.

127

Party Napkins

OBJECTIVES socialization, art training, and developing small muscles.

MATERIALS one plain paper napkin for each child, green construction paper, colored paper scraps, paste or white glue, and scissors for each child.

A plain paper napkin can be made into a special Christmas party napkin easily. Just fold the napkins however you might ordinarily do it. In advance, cut a supply of tall green triangles from construction paper. Give each child a "triangle tree" to paste on his or her napkin.

Let the children use paper scraps to cut tiny circles to paste on the trees for decorations. Then paste or glue them to the napkins. Collect the napkins, and save them for the Christmas party. If you wish, you can write the children's names on the napkins as you collect them. Then, on the special day show the children how to place the Christmas napkins to the left of their place mats.

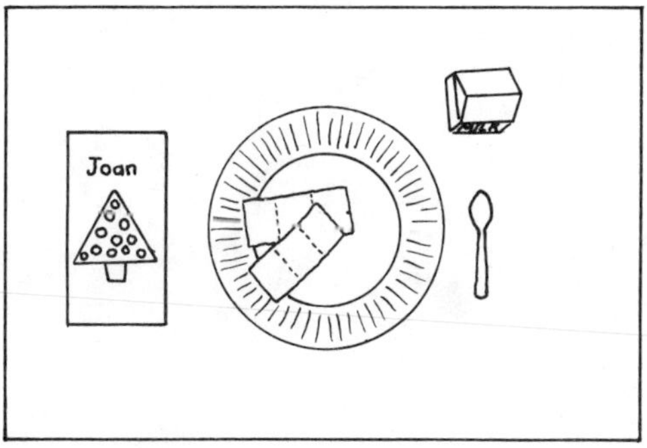

variations

Instead of cutting the decorations from scrap paper, put star stickers on the trees.

On Thanksgiving, paste turkey stickers on plain napkins.

For Valentine's Day, paste red construction-paper hearts on pink or white napkins.

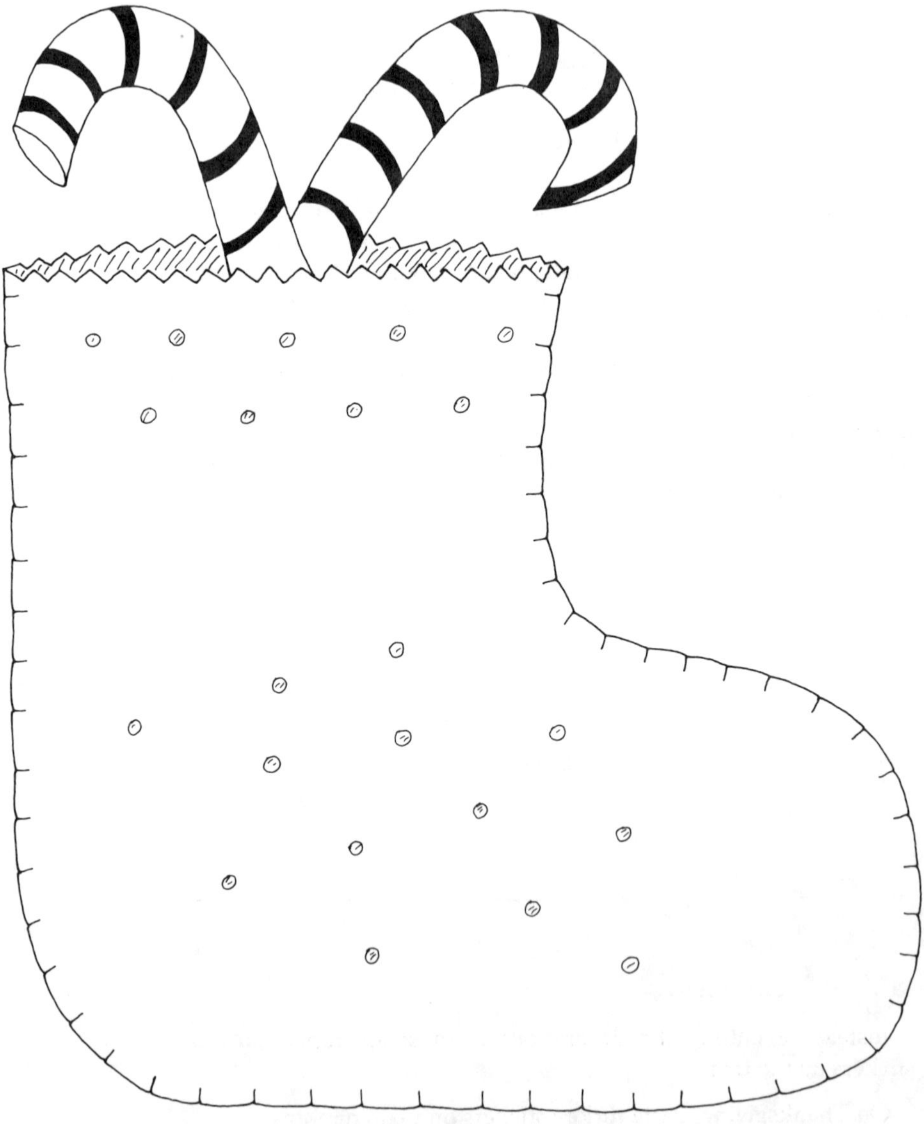

128

From Me to You

OBJECTIVE a Christmas gift from teacher to child.

MATERIALS red or green felt (one yard makes twenty-five stockings), sequins, candy canes, pinking shears, needle, embroidery thread, and glue.

Some teachers like to give little Christmas gifts to each child in their classes. One idea would be to make little felt Christmas stockings, decorate them with bright sequins, and fill them with Christmas candy.

Make a pattern something like the illustration, about $4\frac{1}{4}$ inches high and 5 inches wide from heel to toe. Cut two pieces of felt for each stocking. (You might cut the tops with pinking shears.) Sew the stockings together using a blanket stitch, and glue sequins on at random.

Valentine's Day

129

Valentine Post Office

OBJECTIVE socialization.

MATERIALS red and white construction paper, black felt pen, scissors, white glue, and a brown paper lunch bag for each child and the teacher.

Set aside a large bulletin board during February for a Valentine's Day post office. Use either a red background and white letters or the reverse. Use pink, white, red, or lacy hearts for decorative accents.

With a black felt pen print each child's name on a brown paper sandwich bag. Let the children decorate their own bags by pasting small red and white hearts on them, being careful not to cover their names. To speed the project, have enough construction-paper hearts cut in advance.

Open up the bags and attach their backs to the bulletin board with thumbtacks.

TIME-SAVER: It will save you time if class valentines are signed but not addressed. You might write to parents explaining this in a note like the one below.

Dear Parents,

Valentine's Day is almost here, and your child will probably want to give Valentine's cards to members of the class. We have 26 children in our class. And we will be dropping our cards in our Valentine Post Office Thursday morning.

Please let your child sign his or her name to each valentine but do not address the cards to individual children. This will save me a great deal of time in sorting. We will simply drop one valentine into each sack in our Valentine Post Office.

Thank you for your cooperation.

Sincerely,

130
Learning to Cut Valentines

OBJECTIVE developing small muscles.

MATERIALS several tracing forms, felt pen, pencils, scissors, construction paper.

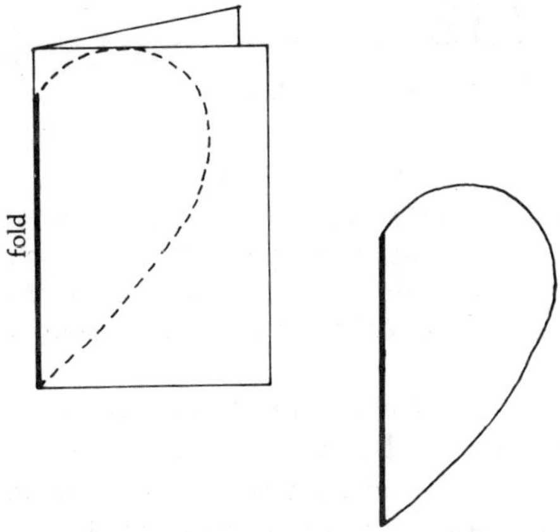

This is a difficult project for many children, yet they are eager to learn and delighted when they master the technique. One way to teach this skill is for you to make tagboard tracing forms. The form should be the shape of half a Valentine heart. The side to be placed on the fold should be heavily colored with felt pen.

You can give each child a folded piece of construction paper, or you can show them how to fold their own papers. Then demonstrate how to place the tracing form on the paper. Explain that they must be sure the colored line lies along the fold of the paper. When the form is traced, they cut out the doubled paper along the lines. When they open it up, they will see a complete valentine.

131
Wrapping-Paper Hearts

OBJECTIVE developing small muscles.

MATERIALS Valentine wrapping paper, tissue paper, scissors, and stapler.

For three-dimensional valentines use valentine gift wrap in printed patterns, solid colors, or foil. Cut two large hearts the same size. Lightly stuff them with tissue paper, and staple them together.

132

Yummy Valentines

OBJECTIVE developing small muscles.

MATERIALS 2 large marshmallows for each child (one to eat and one to use for the project), red construction paper, white glue, scissors, crayons, pans of water, and one or two boxes of red gelatin dessert powder.

Cut a red valentine heart from 9″ x 12″ construction paper, one for each child. (This can be done in advance.) Give each child a heart, and have the children make faces on their valentines with crayons, leaving blank spaces where the noses would be.

When the faces are done, give each child a large marshmallow. Explain that they aren't to eat this one, but when they finish their valentine faces, you have some extras you will give them. Provide small pans of water for wetting the marshmallows slightly on all but one round surface. Demonstrate. Then, have the children wet their marshmallows and roll them in red gelatin dessert powder. Let dry. Then, using a tiny spot of glue, place the sparkly marshmallow on the valentine face, where it becomes a yummy valentine nose.

variation

Instead, the children could make a tray of sparkly valentine marshmallows (without faces) to serve at their party.

133
"Be My Valentine" Game

OBJECTIVE developing auditory discrimination.
MATERIALS one construction-paper heart (about 4" x 5").

Cut a small paper valentine heart, and select one child to sit in the middle of the floor, and have the other children sit in a circle around that child. While the child in the middle has his or her eyes closed, another child quietly takes the valentine that is lying next to him or her and returns to the edge of the circle, where all the children place their hands behind their backs. The child who took the valentine says, "Be my valentine." The child in the center opens his or her eyes and tries to guess which one has the valentine. If the guess is right, that child stays in the circle for the second round. If the guess is wrong, the child who has the valentine becomes the guesser in the middle of the circle.

variation

Change "A Tisket, a Tasket" to a Valentine's Day game by dropping a valentine instead of a handkerchief.

March and April

134
From Valentines to Shamrocks

OBJECTIVE developing small muscles.
MATERIALS green construction paper, scissors, paste or white glue, and background paper for each child.

Usually in March children are still enthusiastic about cutting

valentine hearts. Use this enthusiasm to advantage by having them cut green paper in place of red. Have each child cut three green valentines, and then demonstrate how they can "magically" turn the green valentines into Saint Patrick's Day shamrocks by arranging them in clusters, as shown here, and pasting them on background sheets. Stems can be made from the green scraps.

135
variation
Saint Patrick's Day Cards

Fold sheets of 9" x 12" white drawing paper in half for Saint Patrick's Day cards. Paste shamrocks on the fronts, and print the messages inside.

136
variation
March Folders

The children can make folders to take their March work papers home in. Fold 12" x 18" sheets of drawing paper in half, and staple up their sides. Children can paste shamrocks on the fronts and print the word *March* along with their own names.

137

Snake Magic

OBJECTIVE developing muscles.

MATERIALS none.

This game might be played on or around Saint Patrick's Day, when the children are learning something about the origins of the day.

Choose one child to be King Snake. King Snake collects all the other children behind him, except one. That child is Saint Patrick. The rest of the children line up behind King Snake, hanging onto each other's waists. They are the little snakes.

Saint Patrick chases the wiggling, weaving line of snakes and tries to tag the last little snake in the line. When the little snake is tagged, the child goes behind Saint Patrick and hangs onto his waist and becomes a child again.

The game continues until all of the snakes have been turned back into children.

138

In Like a Lion . . .

OBJECTIVE developing small muscles.

MATERIALS three small paper plates for each child, crayons, paste or glue, scraps of yellow construction paper for lions' tails, scraps of black construction paper for lambs' legs and tails, one lamb's head prepared by the teacher with construction paper for each child, cotton balls, and scissors.

Discuss the old description of March as coming in like a lion and going out like a lamb. Make observations on the way March came in this year. Then make some lions and some lambs.

LIONS

Color two small paper plates yellow for each lion. Use one for a head and the other for a body. Paste them together, as illustrated. Use a brown crayon to make the features on the head. Streak the ridges of the top paper plate with brown to resemble the lion's mane. Paste the tail (made from scraps of construction paper) on, and the lion is finished.

LAMBS

Glue white cotton balls on a paper plate for each lamb, as shown. Demonstrate, to help children know how much glue to use. Then, let them glue on prepared construction paper heads, tails, and two legs each. (The children can make legs and tail from black construction-paper scraps.) They can use black crayon to draw on an eye.

You can arrange the lions and lambs on a bulletin board titled, "IN LIKE A . . . " on one side and "OUT LIKE A . . . " on the other. Let the children decide which sides lions and lambs should go on this March.

139
April Fool

OBJECTIVE developing language.

MATERIALS none.

Children enjoy playing April Fools' Day jokes, and they provide a good opportunity for language development. You might begin by playing a simple April Fools' joke on the children, such as, "Look boys and girls, there is a chicken at our window!"

Explain a little of the history of April Fools' Day. Tell the children that it is a very old custom, and all kinds of people like to play jokes on their friends on this day. It is thought that spring has something to do with it. People begin to feel foolish and frisky as the weather gets nicer.

In France the victims of April Fools' jokes are called April fish. In Scotland they are called gawks or cuckoos, but in many English-speaking countries, they are April Fools.

Ask the children to remember an April Fools' joke that they played on someone or one that someone played on them. They can take turns telling about them.

If children can't remember any jokes, you might help them plan some they can play on their parents when they go home.

140
Spring Stars

OBJECTIVE building a positive self-image.

MATERIALS construction paper for border and umbrella, scissors, and tacks or stapler.

Make a spring bulletin board to display the children's work. Put a scalloped border around the edges. (Construction paper 12" x 18" cut into thirds the long way and scalloped on one edge makes a nice border for a large bulletin board.) Make a three-dimensional umbrella of the same color construction paper as the border. Make it large enough to be the focal point of the bulletin board.

You can make the umbrella by folding two 12″ x 18″ sheets of construction paper in half the long way. Cut across the diagonal making two triangles per sheet, and scallop the bottom of each triangle. Arrange the triangles to form umbrella. Use black construction paper to make a long handle.

Make one star with each child's name printed on it. Scatter them around on the board, and ask the children which pieces of their spring work (one for each child) to post under their stars. They may wish to post good papers under their stars, or they might even draw special pictures.

Some children like to change their papers every day. Others would rather make a collection of papers under their stars before deciding to take them home.

variation

Make a large spring flower for the focal point of the bulletin board and a small flower for each child. Change the title to "SPRING FLOWERS." The children can make construction-paper flowers for the border.

141
Pussy Willows

OBJECTIVES science enrichment and art training.

MATERIALS half a 9″ x 12″ sheet of light blue construction paper per child, a larger sheet of dark blue or black construction paper per child, white poster paint, brushes, black crayons, and scissors.

Make delicate pictures of pussy willows on construction paper with dabs of white paint. Frame them in construction paper of contrasting color, and enjoy them on a spring bulletin board.

First cut 9″ x 12″ light blue construction paper in half so there is half a sheet for each child. Have each child draw a stem with black crayon vertically on the paper. Then show the children how to dab small blobs of white poster paint on either side of their stems with paintbrushes. (Dip the brush gently into a container of white paint. Then, holding the brush in your fist, dab gently one time for each pussy willow blossom.) Let the pictures dry, and frame them on larger sheets of black or dark blue construction paper.

variation

Use the same basic design but, instead of painting, have the children glue grains of puffed rice or puffed wheat on the stems to represent the pussy willow flowers.

142
Clip a Colored Butterfly

OBJECTIVES developing small muscles and decision-making.

MATERIALS one clamp-type clothespin for each child, duplicated butterfly outlines, felt pens, crayons, scissors, clear plastic sandwich bags, and stapler.

Children will enjoy seeing Mom clip this special Mother's Day creation to the edge of the kitchen curtain or the top of a lamp shade.

Give each child a duplicated sheet with one or two butterfly forms on it similar to the example here. (Two butterflies give the children a chance to select their better effort.) Make sure the bodies of the butterflies are as long as a clamp-type clothespin.

Have the children outline each butterfly with a felt-tipped pen. (Black lines look attractive.) Next, suggest that they do their very best coloring on both butterflies. When they finish, they can cut the butterflies out. (Younger children sometimes need help with cutting, but it goes fairly fast.)

Now, have them glue the bodies of the butterflies they have chosen, onto the clothespins.

When the glue is dry, put the butterflies into clear-plastic sandwich bags, and staple across the tops. A little bow or perhaps a colored flower could be added to complete the gift wrapping.

143
The Big Egg

OBJECTIVE developing small muscles.

MATERIALS many pieces of colored tissue paper (about 3" square), white glue, and scissors.

Make a large multicolored Easter egg for the bulletin board, using the wadded paper procedure. Cut the basic big egg from butcher paper, or use smaller pieces of construction paper cut and taped together to make an egg shape large enough to fill your bulletin board.

Then let the children wad up colored tissue paper and glue it on the form until the whole egg is covered. To wad the paper, pinch the center of a square and crumple the loose edges slightly with your free hand. Twist the tight end and dip it into white glue and stick it to the egg form.

variations

You could use the same technique to make a "Great Pumpkin" for Halloween, a "Big Tree" for Christmas, or a "Big Heart" for Valentine's Day.

144

Funny Bunnies

OBJECTIVE reinforcing the concept of the circle.

MATERIALS colored construction paper (one 9″ x 12″ sheet per child for background), construction paper for circles, cotton balls, glue, and black crayons.

Cut circles in advance. Each child will need one 5-inch body, one 3-inch head, and two 1-inch circles for ears and legs.

As the children create funny bunnies, you can reinforce the concept of circle and they can practice their folding and cutting.

Give each child a sheet of bright-colored construction paper for a background. Then distribute the precut circles. Explain that the largest circle will be the bunny's body. Have them glue it in the middles of their papers. Demonstrate approximately where. Explain that the middle-size circle is the bunny's head. Have them glue the head to the body. Then have them cut the remaining small circles in half by folding them first to get the cutting line. Use two halves for the bunny's ears and two halves for the legs, as shown. Have them draw the whiskers with black crayon, and glue a cotton ball on each for the bunnies' tails.

145

Easy Easter Baskets

OBJECTIVE developing small muscles.

MATERIALS one half-pint milk carton for each child, tissue paper, construction paper, white glue, pans, Easter "grass," and jelly beans.

In advance, cut the slanted tops off the milk cartons to make them into boxes. Cut loop handles (about 1″ x 8″) from construction paper and staple them to the boxes. Cut a supply of 2-inch tissue-paper squares.

Give each child a carton with the handle stapled in place. Discuss Easter baskets, and explain that the children are going to decorate their milk cartons and make them into pretty little Easter baskets.

Show the children how to take a tissue-paper square from the supply in front of them and crush it into a loose wad, and then dip it into a small pan of white glue. (Pot-pie tins work well for this, and they can be placed so they will be available for two or three children to use at a time.) When there is glue on the end of the paper wad, the child sticks it onto the milk carton. The object is to cover the sides completely with papers. They may choose to use all one color or many colors. You might make a sample or two to show them how the finished baskets will look.

When everyone is finished, have the children leave their baskets on a table or some other appropriate place. Make sure their names are on the bottoms of their baskets. Then, after the children leave, put Easter "grass" and candy jelly beans in each basket.

146

Pie Plate Egg Hunt

OBJECTIVE developing small muscles.

MATERIALS tissue paper, one pie plate, a drinking straw for each child, and scissors.

For something different in Easter egg hunts, cut several tissue-paper eggs about three inches long. Place the eggs in a pie plate. Give each child a straw. The child whose turn it is puts one end of the straw to his mouth and holds the other end to the pie plate. He takes a deep breath, trying to see how many tissue-paper eggs he can pick up on the end of the straw. The child with the most is the winner.

This is a good game to include in a math center. After they know the game, two or more children can play it without supervision. It gives them extra practice in counting as they help each other find out how many eggs they have on the ends of their straws.

147

Spring Hat Contest

OBJECTIVES developing language and creativity.

MATERIALS paper plates and other materials at home.

Sometime in the spring, announce that the class will have a spring hat design contest. You might explain that some very fine designers are men, and that boys will enjoy designing spring hats, as well as girls.

The children are to make their hats at home, using paper plates for the base. Show them a couple of hats you have decorated, to give them an idea of the possibilities. Encourage them to use all kinds of interesting scraps they find at home.

On the last day of school before spring vacation, each child is to bring his or her creation to school in a paper sack. Set aside a time for the contest, when the children are to model their hats. You might ask the principal and another teacher to act as judges. Prizes might go to the creators of the funniest, the prettiest, and the most unusual hats. You might want to award smaller prizes to the other children, too, because their hats are also very special.

Dear Parents,

We are going to have a spring Hat Design Contest in our room on ___*date*___ at ___*time*___. You are invited to come and share the experience with us.

The children have been asked to design their own hats at home. You may help your child assemble the creation, but please encourage your child to use his or her own ideas in making the actual hat.

A paper plate is to be used as the base. Shoestrings, ribbon, or a scarf can be strung through holes poked in the plate to hold the hat in place.

Prizes will be awarded for the funniest, the prettiest, and the most unusual hats. All of the children will receive some award for their effort.

If you have any questions, please feel free to contact me, and thank you very much for your help.

Sincerely yours,

You might send a short note ahead of time explaining the contest to the parents and inviting them to watch the spring parade.

Before the contest you might enjoy reading aloud the book *Belinda's New Spring Hat* by Eleanor Clymer (New York: Franklin Watts, Inc., 1969).

148

Patchwork Flowers

OBJECTIVES developing small muscles, and reinforcing recognition of geometric shapes.

MATERIALS 12″ x 18″ drawing paper (one sheet for each child); many basic geometric shapes cut from scraps of wallpaper, wrapping paper, tissue paper, felt, fabric, brown and bright-colored construction paper; glue; and scissors.

Let the children help prepare a surprise spring bulletin board. Give each child a 12″ x 18″ sheet of drawing paper. Talk with them about the geometric shapes you have cut ahead of time. Tell them they may choose a large number of the shapes from the precut supply and glue them all over their papers in a design. (You might make a sample to show them what you mean.) Tell the children you will collect their designs when they have finished and make something very special out of them. It will be a surprise.

Later, cut their papers into large patchwork flowers. Cut a large basket out of brown construction paper, and arrange the flowers in and around it on the bulletin board. Label the bulletin board, "WELCOME SPRING."

Gifts to Make

149
Cookbooks for Mom

OBJECTIVE developing language.

MATERIALS a recipe from home from each child, all typed and a set duplicated for each child; construction paper for covers (two per child); crayons; scissors; glue; and stapler; (for wrapping paper, newsprint or finger-painting paper, sponge or drinking straws, poster paint, and pie tins).

Ask each child to bring in a copy of his or her mother's favorite recipe. Type the whole collection of recipes onto duplicate masters (two pages per master), and duplicate them for books for the class.

Let the children decorate construction-paper covers for the books, either with crayons or by cutting out pictures of food and pasting them on in pleasing designs. Staple the books together, and wrap them for Mother's Day or for Christmas.

For gift-wrapping paper give each child a large sheet of newsprint or finger-painting paper. Pour a small amount of poster paint into a pie tin. Give the children sections of sponge to dip into the paint and press onto the paper. Another way of decorating would be to have them use straws and blow circles of paint onto the paper.

150

Wooden Wall Plaques

OBJECTIVES developing art skills and creativity.

MATERIALS small scraps of wood, a piece of paneling or wallboard for each child (about 9″ x 12″), a picture hanger with teeth for each child, white glue, and poster paint or shellac.

Prepare for this activity by collecting small scraps of wood from the school workshop or from a neighborhood lumberyard. The basic plaques can be scraps of paneling or wallboard approximately 9″ x 12″ or smaller, and not necessarily rectangular in shape. Sometimes you can find round pieces of wood, which also make nice plaques. The other scraps should be considerably smaller.

The hardware store has small picture hangers with teeth that you can nail to the back of each base before the project begins.

On the day the children start work, cover the tables with newspaper. Place the container of decorative wood scraps in the middle of the table or on a small table where the children can get them easily. Hand out one bottle of white glue to every two or three students.

Give each child a basic board with its hanger, and explain the idea of gluing scraps of wood on that base in an interesting design. Make sure they do not glue pieces on the back, where the hanger is attached, and show how they can tell which end is the top of the plaque.

Once the children have the directions clear in their minds, let them select two or three pieces of wood at a time. (They may exchange them for other scraps as they go on if they wish.) Ask them first to make the designs without glue. When they have a design that pleases them, then they may glue the pieces carefully in place.

The next day, after the glue is dry, the children can paint their plaques with poster paints or shellac.

151

Perfect Paperweights

OBJECTIVE developing creative thinking.

MATERIALS each child brings in an appropriate rock, poster paint or cutout pictures and glue, and shellac.

Ask each child to bring in a rock that would make a good paperweight. It is a good idea to show an example of one that is approximately the right size (about 5″ long, 2″ wide).

Have them wash and dry the rocks carefully and then paint them or glue pictures on them. When the decoration is dry, shellac the rocks with as many coats as are needed to make them attractive.

Sometimes, with an especially pretty rock, shellac alone is enough to make it a most attractive paperweight.

152

Rock-Hound Bookends

OBJECTIVES developing small muscles and social studies enrichment.

MATERIALS two bricks for each child, many small stones, white glue, felt, and shellac.

Each child will need two bricks and a bag of small stones. Glue the stones to the bricks, leaving one large side and one short end of each brick smooth. Shellac. Felt may be glued to the bottom of each brick so the bricks will not scratch wooden surfaces.

This project could be correlated with a social-studies unit about the state in which you live. You might talk about the types of rocks found in your state and use the rocks on the bookends as examples. It isn't necessary to identify the rocks. With such young children, learning that all states may not have the same types of rocks will be enough of an introduction for later learning.

V

The Last Days of School

The end of a child's first year in school is both happy and sad. It is sad for a child because it is—we hope—the end of a happy, familiar time of joy and learning. It is also happy because it marks a beginning. Basically, this is what genuine growth is all about. It means having the courage and confidence to try new things and, in the process, to let go of the old.

If the children you teach are interested in taking on new challenges, even though they may be a little frightened by them at first, it means that you, their teacher, have had a most successful year.

The ideas in this final chapter are designed to help you wrap up that successful year in ways that will mean something special to you and your children.

153

A Visit into the Future

OBJECTIVES building self-confidence and socialization.

MATERIALS two construction-paper covers and 3″ x 5″ drawing paper and crayons for each child.

Sometime near the end of the school year, plan to visit either the room where the children will go in the fall or else a similar room, if the children will be going to other buildings. Arrange for their next teacher to explain some of the things that will take place in the room when it becomes their room. Ask her to explain some of the things they will be doing, as well as what will be expected of them at that level.

The children might sit at the larger desks or tables. They might observe the older children doing their work or listen as those children tell about their year.

This can be rewarding if your children are the least bit apprehensive about moving from their familiar surroundings. The trip into the future gives them a feeling of importance. It tells them they are growing up and ready to move on.

After the visit, encourage the children to make up a thank-you note.

A BIG THANK YOU

Fold a large sheet of construction paper or finger-painting paper in half for the cover of your thank-you card. Design a simple cover picture, and with the children's help compose a message for the inside.

Then give the children smaller sheets of drawing paper (approximately 3″ x 5″). Have each one draw a picture of himself or herself on it and print his or her name below the picture. Paste all the pictures around the message. Use the back of the thank-you card if you need the space.

When the card is finished, you might select two or three children to deliver the big thank-you note in person.

The Last Day of School

Children enjoy feeling grown-up and independent on the last day of school. By this time the classroom is usually cleaned, toys and materials have been put away for the summer, and vacation is in sight. The following are a few ideas for making this last day of school a very special affair. Select a few of the ideas, and discuss the possibilities with the children. Let them take part in planning their day.

154

All-by-Ourselves Party

Let the children make all the refreshments for their party. One group could make fruit drink. Another could make ice-cream. And a third group could prepare fudge.

FRUIT DRINK

Decide on a flavor of Cool-Aid (or the like) the whole class would enjoy. Decide what supplies you will need—how many packages of drink mix, how much sugar, what kinds of containers for mixing and for drinking, and so on. Discuss using ice, and make arrangements for getting and keeping it. On the day of the party, prepare according to directions on the package.

EASY ICE-CREAM

Combine one quart half-and-half cream, $\frac{3}{4}$ cup sugar, $\frac{1}{8}$ tsp salt, and $1\frac{1}{2}$ tsp vanilla extract in a bowl. Stir until sugar and salt are

completely dissolved. Pour into an electric ice-cream freezer. Freeze until firm (15 to 20 minutes). Makes about 1½ quarts. Ice and salt packed around the container should be from 6 to 8 parts cracked ice to 1 part salt.

QUICK UNCOOKED FUDGE

Melt ¼ cup butter in a saucepan. Stir in ¼ cup condensed milk and 1 tsp vanilla extract. Gradually add a mixture of 1 pound powdered sugar, ¾ cup cocoa, and ¼ tsp salt. Mix until soft and creamy. Press the mixture into a shallow buttered pan or onto wax paper, and cut it into serving pieces.

155
Field Day

Set up a series of races, games, and tests of skills mastered on the playground equipment, in jumping rope, or in tossing balls.

Make paper ribbons or happy faces to award the winners. Make sure each child wins at least one for his or her efforts.

Serve simple refreshments, such as canned fruit punch and store-bought cookies, outside.

Below are some ideas for events:

SILLY RACES

Establish a starting line and a finish line. The children could run as teams or individually. Call out the kind of Silly Race to be run just before they start. Possibilities are: running backwards, walking fast, hopping, holding their noses, jumping, skipping, holding one ankle, and waddling like ducks.

BROAD JUMP

Set up a starting line and have the children try to jump as far as they can. Tell them to freeze where they land until everyone has had a turn. The one who jumps farthest is the winner. This can be set up in groups to keep children from jumping on each other and to yield more winners.

RELAY RACES

Divide the children into three or four teams, and let them run around a pole, a chair, or some other designated object. (Relays can be difficult to run if the children have not had previous practice during the year.)

156
Peanut Hunt

Have some older children hide a sackful of peanuts in the shell all around the play area. (Make sure the peanuts are not hidden too well. Most of them should be in plain sight.) Give the children a time limit of five or ten minutes. The one who finds the most peanuts is the winner.

157
Play Favorites

Help the children to plan the day around their favorite games, stories, poems, finger plays, and songs. Some children might enjoy retelling their favorite stories. Others might enjoy leading favorite songs or finger plays.

158
Have a Show

Select an enjoyable film to show. Make popcorn to eat from Styrofoam cups while you watch it.

159

Make Summer Forget-Me-Not Books

MATERIALS leftover duplicated sheets from all year, construction paper for covers, felt pens and crayons, and stapler.

During the year, save any leftover duplicated practice pictures and patterns, pages from workbooks, and the like. On the last day of school, each child can make a collection from among the pages you have saved. Staple the collections together inside simple construction-paper covers, and suggest the children print their names on the fronts, decorate them with pictures of summer fun—and maybe some of the children will actually do a little summer review work.

You could prepare a note to parents in advance to explain that the Forget-Me-Not Book is not required homework, but just something the children have decided to make so they can play school during the summer, perhaps on a rainy day.

This note would also give you a good opportunity to tell parents how much you have appreciated their help during the school year:

Dear Parents:

Today we put together Forget-Me-Not Books. The children were free to select pages from a variety of sheets left over from the activities we have done this year. This is not homework, and your child may or may not want to complete the exercises in the book. It is a good source of rainy-day or play-school activities for the summer months.

I would also like to take this opportunity to express my appreciation for all of your help during the school year. I would especially like to thank Mrs._______ and Mrs._______who served as homeroom mothers.

I have enjoyed having your child in my class this year, and I feel we have all had a very successful experience.

Thank you again, and do have a pleasant summer.

Sincerely yours,

Index of Activities

The numbers following each entry identify activities. They are not page numbers.